Travels
with a
Two Piece

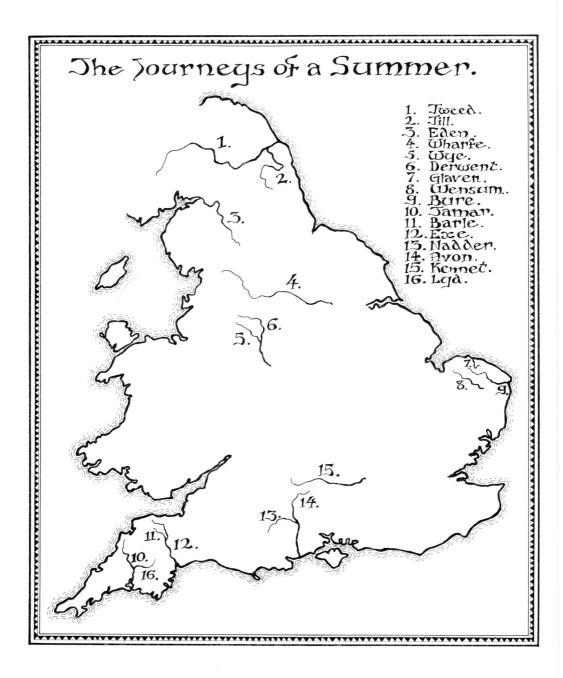

The Journeys of a Summer.

1. Tweed.
2. Till.
3. Eden.
4. Wharfe.
5. Wye.
6. Derwent.
7. Glaven.
8. Wensum.
9. Bure.
10. Tamar.
11. Barle.
12. Exe.
13. Nadder.
14. Avon.
15. Kennet.
16. Lyd.

TRAVELS WITH A TWO PIECE

JOHN BAILEY

Illustrated by Chris Turnbull

THE CROWOOD PRESS

First published in 1985 by
The Crowood Press
Crowood House
Ramsbury
Marlborough
Wiltshire SN8 2HE

British Library Cataloguing in Publication Data

Bailey, John
Travels with a two piece
1. Grayling fishing – Great Britain 2. Trout fishing – Great Britain
I. Title
799.1'755 SH91.G7

ISBN 0–946284–27–X

Typeset by Inforum Limited, Portsmouth
Printed and bound in Great Britain by
Redwood Burn Limited
Trowbridge, Wiltshire

Contents

To Robbie, Jack and Peter, and all who care for trout rivers

Acknowledgements

In the East, I would like to thank above all Robbie and Peter Suckling. They are both men who have helped lift trout fishing into something remarkable in this area, in rivers where the art had fallen back a very long way indeed. I cannot possibly express my thanks, or their due from the sport itself, for their time and generosity. I would also like to thank John Oxenford for the permission to use his letter.

In the South, I would above all thank Reelscreamer, and his father, who between them did so much to help me into the chalk stream apprenticeship. Reelscreamer has been a very positive influence throughout the book – I have always imagined I was writing it for him, almost, alone. I would also like to thank my friend John Dennis for the occasional days on his water, and to a flyfisher lady who I admired from afar.

In the West, I must thank the proprietors and staff of the Tarr Steps Hotel and the Arundell Arms Hotel. Above all I owe a great debt to my childhood hero, a traveller, who, in part, inspired the spirit of this book.

In Derbyshire, I thank the manager of the Cavendish Arms, the estate manager at the Chatsworth Estate, and the river keepers of that area, Tom Richardson especially, who struck me as one of the most river caring men that I have met.

In the North, I would thank Mr Bedford-Payne, a man full of goodwill, generosity, and very well met. I owe a special debt to a Mr Pape who is amongst the nicest fly fishermen I met – and I suspect is the best, which is a tribute, for I have met very good ones indeed. I must thank Mr and Mrs Brooks Sykes of the

Tillmouth Park Hotel who run about the most beautiful fishing hotel known to man, or to me at least.

In the end, I would thank Harry who gave me the two piece – a rod which has never let me down – and whom I hope I have not disgraced by this book.

Preface

It so happened in the summer of 1984 that I found myself free, or pretty well so, for twelve weeks. Free. Free from traditional cares of the everyday man. Free to enter into any fantasy that I wished. Above all, free to fish. And if need be, to travel to my fish. The dreams I have whirled in my pillow hours flooded in: a summer in Spain to put a hook into one of the great barbel I had seen there during travels in the 1960s: free to travel to India, to play a gold-plated Mahseer in coffee water, knowing the elephants would never forget me: able to travel North, on a route through Finland I had been given, where I could cast to grayling and char in the bottle-green waters somewhere above latitude sixty: I could look for the leviathan carp that, rumour has told, come out of France, somewhere between the Alps Maritime and the Cote D'Azur. And if I am dreaming, why could I not hunt a beluga, the emperor of sturgeon, in the Black Sea, or the Caspian or to whatever deltas the tales take me.

So the wild mind travelled, and does still on wet nights when the fire broods all day, and the dead leaves knock against the window as they fall into the earth.

And yet, free though I was, what I did was to head into the valleys of England, with a two ounce rod, content for trout and the odd grayling. Freedom for a little English summer, bordered in by hedgerows, woods, lanes and old farm tracks; a summer of villages, market towns, and keepers' cottages; a green summer of water weeds, long grasses, of willow leaves; a summer of peaceful reflection, of happy affection. A summer when once again I grew to love England, to treasure her all over again.

[11]

But if there were a purpose behind these long hot days (for it was a summer of serious drought) more than enjoyment, then it was to see how and where trout lived in English rivers. Catching a fish was pleasant. It was never essential. I wanted to watch them, involve myself in their behaviour.

So many things caught my eye as I went: a certain fish in a certain lie; a certain fish's feeding habits; certain beautiful days in special places; certain fishermen, brilliant as anglers, wonderful as human beings – for the one is no good without the other. Anything I saw, or caught, or learnt, or felt, 'or wondered, went into my notebooks. Went in at once, as soon as the impact exploded into my world. There are some dozen, full now, full of this one rich summer, of its memories, of sketches of a rock pool or of a weeded lie or the way a sea trout jumped on its way to the stars. Put them all together and there is how the world looked to me this summer long.

In writing this book, these notebooks are the core, the memory bank. All I do now is to try to put more smoothly the jumble of thought and experience, to draw the threads together.

And yet, it is important, I feel, to remain true to the spirit of the notes. If all the rough edges were to go, then no more would this be a book written on the river bank, under sunshine, in moonlight, on pages damp from mist and dew, crumpled from confinement in tackle bag or game pocket, smelling of that waterland of trout, weeds and cowslip banks.

I did not feel this was a book best illustrated by photography, even though I had a camera with me and have now a thousand prints on record. The glimpses into fish behaviour I witnessed cannot help but come across poorly on a single frame sequence. The lies I treasured do not seem clear on photographs, somehow always out of context with their surroundings: either you put the whole valley in frame and the lie is lost, or you focus on the lie itself and then shut out the all important setting. Fish I caught look, on film, stiff stark things. I grin in triumph I do not really feel: I am remembering the showers of spray the camera has ignored. The valley hideaway I loved for its subtleties of tone and shade, for the warmth that got to my very soul, becomes, on an

'eight by six', just another pretty place in the country.

I have worked for several years with Chris Turnbull. By anyone's standards he is a very fine fisherman. He knows instinctively how a fish looks, and how rivers 'feel'. He has been there, he has done it all himself, he is an outdoor artist and he has the ability to convey these impressions through his drawings. Also he knows me. He knows what in my stumbling prose, I am searching to say and with his art he can come to my aid and help me through.

Over the last two decades, angling literature has taken new turns. It is now a literature dominated by the *how to*: how to fish reservoirs, how to fish from boats, how to tie flies, how to cast and how to be successful at all costs. But angling is a more complex sport than this trend suggests. It should be a passion, a way of living with far more objectives than success alone. Older writers and, I believe, older fishermen drew more out of their waterside lives by smelling the roses along their way. Whilst I hope some useful things will be drawn from my book, what I really hope is that readers will agree how fortunate we are in still having a green England, lovely rivers and entrancing, beautiful fish that on very special days, we might even catch.

Itteringham.
October 1984.

Early Travels

I do not come new to a summer of travelling for my fish. It began with me early and the habit has stayed, for, in some ways, our childhood is a completion as well as a beginning, and I do not feel that the essence of my pleasures has changed much, if at all. Certainly my love for rivers and for trout was born long ago, on a midsummer evening, when the month was July, or maybe August, and the days had not yet become tired-eyed.

The weather had been warm with sunlight since the early afternoon and the wind had dropped away to a breath, a hush, to nothing at all. I had a rod by me, but I was walking and then sitting and watching. I was on a river, and that is the point, either fishing or not. It was a river to the last degree of perfection, flowing from the West so that it was possible to look along it towards the setting sun. I saw a moving, shimmering stream of gold. There was a haze above it, a zone of tiny, shining stardust particles that fascinated me: of pollen that cascaded from the trees: of billion upon billion insects, dancing, loving, falling back to be absorbed into the lacquered film of water, to be lost for evermore.

A mile of water hurried past me, never stopping, never breathless: a host of insects had been and gone forever but the trout over the gravels had never moved. I saw a fish feeding under an alder tree, another between the stepping stones and a kingfisher on the arch of a footbridge. I knew I would not rather be anywhere else on earth.

When I was eleven, my parents did for me this special thing, to send me alone, but for my rods, on a train to a hotel by a Welsh

Border river. This was my first taste of full twenty-four hour freedom. I had never been allowed to lie in bed until the late morning, or have breakfast at lunchtime, and lunch for dinner, and I need never have had a bath the whole week long for all anybody cared. Nobody before had ever bought me a drink in a bar and no adult had ever asked my advice seriously until then, when in a minor way I became known as a river expert.

My emotions were laid waste. An elderly artist devoted all lights of the sun and moon to show me where beauty lay and how I could look for it. I learnt to comfort myself when I fell and bled from a rock downstream and I fell in love with the young manageress who took me to a concert in the local town: there is a scar of fingernail width on the point of my chin now and there will always be a snatch of Chopin that leaves me wistful whenever I hear it on a late night show.

In such a valley of mystery and of total happiness, my passion for fishing grew. Never before had I fished all night, or heard the otters whistle or been so aware of the dance of moonbeams. I had never seen water look silver, not blue, nor had I watched dawn break or been out in the fields and woods and felt the dew falling around me.

The river never left me that week. It wound around the village,

past the hotel, under my bedroom so that I could hear it whilst I slept. The water had melted from the snows at two and three thousand feet and ran ice cold and clear, and bred hardy, clean fish. Trout seemed as if to hang in air and the sun cast a shadow as distinct as a man's. No taint hid their colour, their chalk white mouths, the vivid red gills that flared through the covers as they chewed, their buttercup bellies and their fawn skins, that looked the texture of velvet, spangled all over with droplets of ruby red wine.

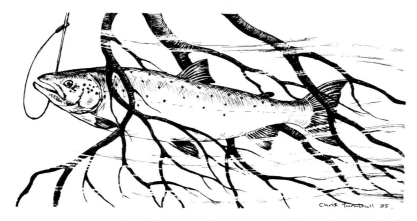

I was intoxicated with trout when I saw a salmon leap at dusk, from a weir through the white water into the glide above. It was a glimpse only, that became a sensation, and then a thrill with both the twilight and the fast water and the thought of greater fish than I had ever imagined.

And, just as the week seemed a fairy story, so it was enchanted with bad angels, and good ones, both of whom laid a claim to my eternal trouting soul. At that time I could hardly say who was the more attractive.

The bad man had a noose of wire, that glowed in the sunshine, and looked like a halo as it hung above the head of a small salmon. He moved it with the cunning of a devil over the fish's cheeks and his eyes glowed like a hawk's. He tightened. His bronzed forearms moved with wicked power and the copper brought blood from the gills of the betrayed fish. He squatted triumphant

[19]

above it and told me to bring it to him, later after nightfall, at a meeting place in the village.

But there was a good man also, who came to look for me at dawn or at dusk, to show me the pinnacle of sport. And, finally, he won. It was the rise of a one pound sea trout on the tail of a pool at dawn that led me his way. I was shown that the splash of a wild fish coming through the mists out of nowhere, the sudden charge of electricity down the line and the wrench of the rod were fine things in themselves, and that whatever successes came thereafter were a bonus.

So, if one week could give me so much, I wondered what ten could do. This present summer of travels was born years ago.

The Two Piece

The summer journey was made somewhat special by the rod that I used on all but a few occasions. It was old, perhaps a hundred years even, about eight and a half feet, and took a number six floating line in its stride. The corks of the butt had been badly nibbled by mice over the years, but the marks smoothed out under fine sand paper, and, best of all, the rod had retained its shape well. By re-whipping 'top to bottom' I straightened out the slight set entirely.

I was given it by an old man on the estate. It had belonged to his father, a man he had never seen, killed in The Great War. I had written a story on the history of the rod which the old man had liked, and as his use of the wand was limited, it became mine. Oh yes, a carbon creation would have done as well, or even better perhaps, but the soul of the two piece I loved. It was willing. It forgave bad casts and it was softly actioned for close in work. Anyway, the object of the summer was not merely to catch fish. I felt it a pleasant thing to restore the old rod, to take it back to the trout streams it was intended for and then retire it for ever. The two piece had been much abused in its long life . . .

★   ★   ★

There is a pool three meadows from my house, as round as a cartwheel and no deeper than the average duck; but wildies flourish there and will always feed, even in mid November. Today was bleak with a fierce wind coming off the beet fields and

[21]

sneaking round the haystacks, and I could not bring myself to fish before the mid afternoon. The late day, late year sun was very bright in the wind swept sky and you could almost sense old Jack Frost up there, waiting to slide down to earth, so I was surprised that I was not to fish alone. Henry, the elderly man I knew so well from the pub, was there.

'I didn't know you fished, Harry,' I said.

'That I only do once in awhile when I get a bit of time,' he replied, 'but I do like to exercise the rod if I can once a year on this day.'

'On this day,' I queried, 'surely it's a bit late on for the wildies.'

'Remembrance Sunday. I had a father that died in 1916. I never knew him in fact, and about all he did for me was to leave me this rod.'

We stared along its length in silence and concentrated on the quill float for some while, and then he told me the tale of the two piece.

It seems that a long time back in an Edwardian summer a young man, more strictly a teenager, went to France for the first time. He took a case of clothes, wore a stiff new suit and carried a light split cane rod that was as well made and very much its owner's delight. From Paris he caught the afternoon train to Tours, entranced all the journey by the wide open plains of sunset France that were so unlike his industrial Yorkshire with its dark grime-stained valleys.

He was met by Robert and his parents, then taken by cart to a farm deep in the Indre-Loire countryside. The blanched August dust billowed up from the horses hooves into his already tired eyes, and the poplar avenues seemed to lead into forever in the lad's mind. But they arrived at the small white building and, being as it was summer, he had the attic room that looked over the small yard and had doves nesting in the gables and a wasp's nest in the skylight.

The window faced east so that the sunrise, the cock of the yard and the cleaning of the churns all coincided to wake him, and with his first glance he took in all the farm, the meadows that cradled a pond and, further away, a river looping lazily along its

[22]

broad valley. Totally in love with the place and very nervous, he took himself down for his first French breakfast.

It seemed an endless summer. Robert was just a little older and infinitely more experienced and showed him all about brandies and wine in the cellar rooms. There was work to be done – animals to look after and the harvest to get in – but none of it seemed hard after a Pennine life. And though they were now Republican farmers, the whole family kept a rich, warm outlook that was left over from their Parisian forbears of the Second Empire and which alternatively shocked and delighted a boy brought up in strict non-conformist drabness.

The two piece got the heaviest work of all. He tried the Cher, the great river beyond the hay meadows, but caught nothing but quite familiar roach. The pond, though, was something different. It was full of long, lean common carp – wildies, we would say now – that went for any bait, if it were big enough, and then scrapped like a miner on a lock-out. Remember that seventy years ago any carp in England was an event; so think how the boy felt to catch a score in a month and you have the picture. He developed a sureness of touch that could guide them through the weeds, away from the branches of the chestnut tree and even coax them from the lily beds themselves. On the farm, they began to call him the Magician.

And there was Dominique – Robert's slightly younger sister. There was a love affair that summer, but it developed so slowly as almost never to happen. Henry gave me very little to go on about the girl, other than she was dark with something quite special about her eyes. Anyway, summer lengthened out until the last night of the boy's stay came around. He was down on the pond, but the fishing was poor and occasionally a shudder of cooler breeze sent a shower of leaves into the water around his float. As always, now, Dominique sat with him. The last week or two they had held hands and, though he missed bites because of it, he cherished the slow, still clumsy kisses. That last night though, something really happened down on the river plain, in the dark, as the mist began to creep over and hide the farmhouse lights from them. The knowledge of it made his head swim as he

[23]

walked back to the now sleeping house, the rod over one arm and his darling, darling Dominique's waist encompassed in the other.

Years on and by now he was married, a qualified man in Bradford with no time for fishing even on a Sunday, but happy even so. But things as they were in 1914 he became a lieutenant in the expeditionary force and was one of the first over to France. After a short training, he was back on the ferry to Calais. His case had gone, the suit would never have fitted now, but he took the same two piece cane rod – partly out of sentiment, partly for good luck and partly because, as an angler, you never know, do you?

It really was a miracle that he was back for leave during December 1914 and for others all through 1915. October 1915 and a baby was conceived and the thought of it sustained him for a long time back in the trenches. June 1916 and his next leave was due – in time for the birth, it seemed – but great things were being planned in the mind of Earl Haig and his time off was cut to just five days. Two days to Bradford and two days back would leave him barely twenty-four hours before returning to only Satan, the black angels and Haig knew what. It was then, probably amongst kit and bandages and shells, so strangely out of place, that the rusted glint of brass ferrule caught his eye and hooked his mind.

Some warm days coincided with the memories of Robert, the carp, the Cher . . . and dear Dominique. June 26th found him on a train heading not North, but West into deeper France. Strange how, away from the Front, the country seemed to be moving at the same slow pace he remembered from eight years before. On that journey the evening light that he knew so well threw long shadows over the figures in the field, but it was with shock that he realised all the workers were women: French manhood was being bled white in the defence of Verdun and there could be nobody left but the women for the land.

It was dark in the city of Tours but he found the hotel at which he and Robert had stayed and the next day he hired a motor cycle with a gallon of petrol and drove out on the old road to the farm. He found it deserted. The shutters were up. Chickens still scratted but the cows had gone along with the plough horses and the pigs. The meadow to the pond was rougher and ungrazed but the water itself seemed preserved from a dream, to the last lily bed, to the rod rest carved for him by Robert and hammered like Excalibur into the clay bank around the sluices. He sat behind it, cast out a red quill and sank uncontrollably into tears.

The carp had gone back a bit in size now that there was nobody to drain off the lake and take the smaller fish away to the table, but he had one of nearly ten pounds, he reckoned, and several of around five, whilst even the smallest would have made the Bradford lads sit up. It was sunset when the owl began to call again and when he lost the best fish of the day into the lily bed that he had always feared. That guiding touch had gone over the years. He felt less like a magician now.

A figure had appeared in front of the house. He knew it was Dominique whilst he was still far away on the meadows, despite the dusk, despite the years: he knew from her walk towards him, from her hair she still kept long. They talked in French: the parents had died, within six months of each other before the War,

[25]

and Robert was shot dead at Ypres. She was married and her husband had been at Verdun . . . Anyway, the old life had gone forever as once more the Prussians had come to wreck a civilisation they could not understand. Before they reached the farm they were hand in hand again as they trod the same old path, and once more they entered the bedroom in the attic.

When he returned to the Front on the Somme his mail waited. Letters from Bradford, and the first photograph of his first son. He looked at them with reddened eyes and slept for a few fitful hours until he was called at dawn on 1 July 1916. At 7.30 a.m. eleven British divisions clambered from their trenches along a thirteen mile front. A mere six German divisions faced them, in deep dugouts though, and machine-gunned their attackers who walked towards them in orderly rows or stood puzzling in front of uncut wire. 110,000 British attacked and over a half were killed or wounded in that single morning. Henry's father of so few hours was one of the 20,000 who lay dying, crying out for days afterwards in the waste called No Man's Land.

'Anyway,' said Henry, 'during the next German war I met up with Dad's Captain. His best friend it seems. By '39 he was a Colonel and he figured me out as soon as he saw me. It was quite a shock to him. He said I seemed like a ghost walking out of 1916. We had dinner. He told me what I've just said and he gave me this here.'

Harry waggled the badly set two piece rod. It had not been re-whipped but the ferrules were polished bright and the corks had been refitted – where the rats had had them. 'It still does, you see, to catch wildies from a pond, and that's how he'd have liked to see it used.'

It would be nice to say Harry caught a carp that evening before the sun finally disappeared, but he didn't. The sky deepened from pinks and blues into a starlit velvet and we left in silence for home.

THE EAST

An Introduction

The glory of Norfolk is locked in its great landed estates, in the wonderful halls with fine porches, mellowed red brick facades, turreted gables, mullioned windows and lilied moats and ha-has; in the estate villages, with the bell towers, the stable yards, the keepers' cottages, the lodges covered in honeysuckle and the walled gardens of old asparagus beds and stately vines; in the beehives buried in the orchards, in the dove cotes, the summer houses, the chestnut mares and the Jersey cows plagued by the flies from the long hay; in the clipped hedgerows of yew and privet, in pleached fruit trees and limes, and in the ancient oaks of the great deer parks. Though the world has changed around them, though the life of the twentieth century has hammered at their walls and gates, many still survive, independent in the traditional family line.

They all have lakes. Sheets of water designed and built for beauty in the future – moon shaped pools, willowed islands that weep in the breeze, old boathouses, thatch reflections in the water, red brick dam walls and legions of reed that fire in the setting sun. They hold tench, smooth skinned olive fish that porpoise at dusk, and rudd that glow golden scaled with fins of flame; some have carp that grow large as young boys and wallow in the silt and weed for over half a century. There are perch that bristle and fight and bite on the worms dangled by the estate children. And there are bream as big as dustbins and pike that the keepers swear could swallow a goose.

But there is one estate that not only has a lake, the most

fabulous of all to my mind, where I have caught mirror carp of twenty pounds and which is sheltered by oaks and copper beeches, but also owns four miles of river. When I first walked there with my fly rod in 1969, I do not think I had ever felt myself so close to a heaven on earth. I was a first year undergraduate then, free from the city for the entire summer by early June, just as the mayfly were in full show. The river as it ran clear and swift over sand and gravel was bursting with life and it seemed that all the happiness of the world poured into that dancing stream and its brave bold trout.

The banks were a wilderness for the estate had long since given up on all sporting activities but the pheasants and the hounds, and there were lies I could never reach for the brambles and bracken and willow herb. All that summer I never saw another soul with a rod and I felt that the meagre stocking that had taken place to supplement the native fish had all been for my benefit alone.

I soon settled on my favourite beats. One was at the top of the estate where the park track humped over a narrow bridge. Beneath unfurled a long slow pool deep in a thick oak wood full of silence and sleeping owls. I never failed to pick up a trout at the tail of this pool, just at the point where it shallowed under an alder, just where the trout was on the verge of invisibility. Another foot upstream and they would have been lost in the deeps and yet a foot more downstream and they would have been glaringly obvious and insecure. No, they always lay in the mid position, where they were just a suspicion, where you thought you saw a fish and then invariably realised that you did. As soon as I had taken one trout from that lie, another would have filled the gap within an hour, but the secret of its desirability I never discovered.

From there the river wound a way over open flood meadows, deeps and shallow quick straights until it entered a wood, nearer the house here, near enough to hear the clock chime and the dogs wailing for their food or freedom. The river was slowing all the time, with more roach appearing in the pools and where the foxy faced pike sneered coldly out of every tree root hole.

But this place also held the biggest trout, happy to eat a dace or two and still have room for a fly feast at dusk. I lost one in July and another, even bigger, in the darkness of a late September day as the season was about to end, as I was about to return to the city. Walking back that night I felt a real desolation; I felt I was leaving the trout river I had always been destined for, where I was made aware of senses I never knew I possessed. It was a place where for that one summer I returned totally to the days of my childhood which were spent wholly in the outdoors; fishing, or hunting foxes with my hammer or later with the one-legged man who had dogs and a gun.

Over the next few years, the fishery became more popular and it was usual to meet three or four anglers up and down the river on a fine day. The estate realised the economic potential and the stocking increased, paths were cut, car-parks hacked out of the woodland, and the coarse fish were netted out and removed. It was still very beautiful and the charm of the estate remained, but it was no longer the lost domain that had captured my soul, and I went less and less to fish there.

In June 1978 I did go back, however, and found the river just as it had been when I first knew it. The car-park was lost in weed. No man could tell where the paths had led and only a few benches here and there told of the day ticket years. The roach, dace and snaggle toothed pike had returned and once more the trout were native browns born on gravel under watercress and not in pens of concrete and steel.

Though I had my money ready for the water keeper when I met him, I had the uneasy feeling all day that I was not where I should be any longer. So it turned out. Some estate workers saw me and called out. The fishing had been stopped and as it was quite private now, I would have to leave. They were only doing their job, they said. I returned to the top wood again in my paradise lost and refound and lost again in a single instant.

But I had fished nearly one whole stolen day and the oaks were throwing their shadows right across the alder lie where a trout was sipping olives as though time had never passed for me. Even had it meant a life sentence, I could not pass him by, even though I did have the honesty to return him, probably to drive away the

[31]

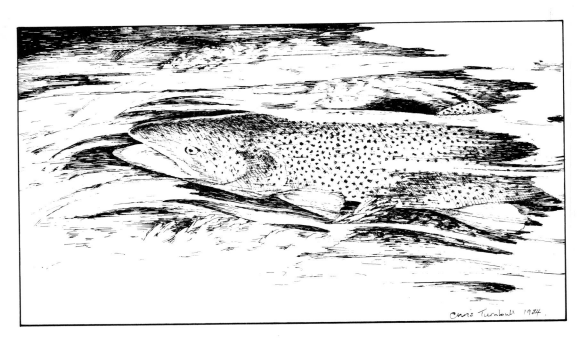

Chris Turnbull 1984.

next in line who had already stepped into his shoes.

And so my introduction to Norfolk river trout fishing ends. But not quite, for this summer, 1984, I returned to the estate, simply to walk, to recapture the old feelings and places for this piece. The whole valley is now one huge gravel pit complex. Where I used to walk and fish is now a maze of pumps, heavy machinery, site huts and banks of spoil and sludge. The wetlands have gone, the woods have gone, and most strange, that winding bright gravel stream is gone. I did find it at last. It has been re-routed, pressed hard against the far side of the valley. It has been straightened and deepened like a dead canal, fit for a roach perhaps, but never again will there be an alder tree with a trout beneath it. Sadly, the domain is lost forever.

The Glaven

This evening, at sunset, I saw four wild peacocks in the wood-land. The throat feathers of the male birds reflected the same iridescence as the bluebells they walked upon, purple swans afloat on the haze of a summer pond. They took fright and made their way over the knoll of ploughland. The sun rolled on its horizon, knocking down church towers, sending the escarpment forest up in flames. A wind was still pushing the clouds south, great plumes of crimson in the sky, shapes of knights and chargers, ruined castles and cannon smoke dragons over all the land. Over me, the peacocks and the trout that still rose under the cherry tree.

The three-quarter moon was up, the sun was down, the peacocks were at roost and the trout had gone, but the image of that sunset remained clear. Realising that nature, this wonderful world, has a soul so real, means I must begin this summer journey of rivers, on the Glaven. The Glaven is not large, not famous, not always crystal clear, not pure chalk, but it is where I would want my river trouting home to be.

This summer the Glaven has become a friend to me. Its spirit is my spirit. Nothing can help but be good there; the evening always seems warm and gentle and I will rise a fish if I remain; where waiting is no hardship – so is the Glaven to me now.

I returned this summer to Hunworth Mill, the point on the Glaven I first knew, and which I loved so much it has drawn me back this year. Then, over a decade ago, the night stretched on nearly to dawn before I made it to my bed in the attic, where I lay awake, mind like the mill race, listening to the river chatter

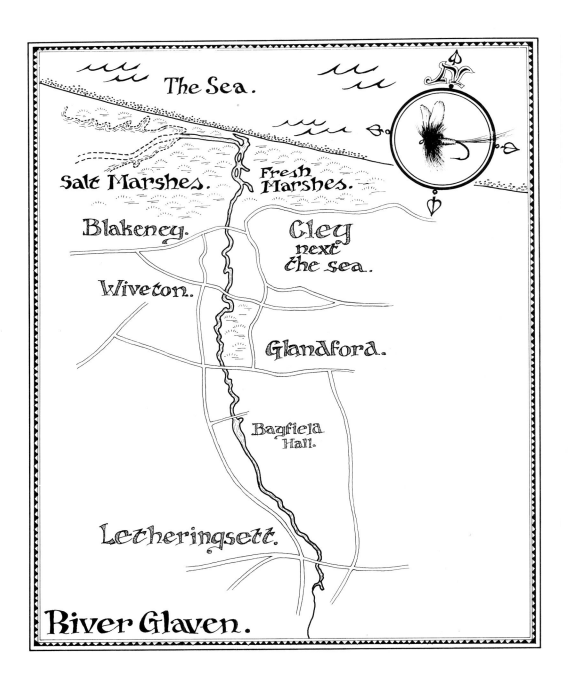

The Sea.

Salt Marshes.

Fresh Marshes.

Blakeney.

Cley next the sea.

Wiveton.

Glandford.

Bayfield Hall.

Letheringsett.

River Glaven.

through the sluice gates, watching the corn store window steal to pewter, grey and pearly blue. Birds began to scuffle under the pantiles. They clawed at the rushes just over my head and one began to sing. I looked outside where it had become very near light. The valley sides were distinct, and the river lay under silks of mist. The moon was fading and no longer threw shadows. There was a lightness in the sky over the downs, and I caught sight of the barn owl coming in home. The short June night had gone. Dawn on a trout river – what was there to do but dress and go fishing?

That bygone morning Hunworth Mill seemed a wondrous

place. G. lived there in those days, and we had a typical under-graduate relationship that can only develop when life is easy and relaxed. He was awake too. He had made up the rods and we went out onto the small mill pond, still hazed, but already dimpled by the upriver brownies.

G. swore by Red Tags and said if we caught any decent fish we would have them for breakfast. We stood on opposite sides of the water that was so tiny we were forced to make alternate casts to avoid tangling. Whenever one hooked a fish it would splash under the other's feet. We returned many too small and fished hard until the sun was over the hill crest to land two good ones which we ate along with the cress from the tail of the pool.

G. left the Mill, left Norfolk, for all I knew. I came back in the following summer vacation to find the place empty and sold. Standing now in the lane outside, looking down the shingle track, listening to the river, all I feel are memories, strong enough to bring me back today. This summer I have had to look out for Glaven trouting of my own.

From Hunworth, the Glaven runs ten miles northwards before it enters the salt marshes and finds its estuary to the sea. There are trout all along its course, small fish, fragile in so tiny a river, as it is upstream. For most of the way, it winds through the farmland valley in miniature pools and runs that can only be fished, if permission can be obtained, with wand-like gear, or hardly even that. It is a river more for the rambler, or the naturalist, the type of man who wanders with a rod and does not care if it remains unused. Along it here lie the acres of thatchers' reed, a windmill, and the street of merchants' houses and sailors' cottages built before the sand and silt barred the way to the North Sea traders' ships.

Below the Mill, two hundred yards or so, stands the round tunnelled railway bridge that once took the north Norfolk line its countrified way to King's Lynn. Now the embankment is overgrown, south facing and a warm place to watch the pheasants in the bracken and a lizard on a stone. Fifty feet beneath runs the Glaven, still a stream, a rod across, but just at the point where a feeder stream enters from the West and creates a shallow gravel ford, a trout waits. An animal track leads to it, travelled by foxes and deer as they roam at night.

Lower down, there are the deep holes in the meadows beneath Ingmote Hill, a ridge of oaks above the lone riverside farmhouse. Then the picket-railed cottage that stands between the strip of common land and the river, and has a trout rising by its door. There is a Jack Russell with a brown ear and a goose that hisses as I move on. At the ford at Little Thornage there is a trout lying in a strange depression in the bed, as though once a tractor tyre sank in deeply there.

[36]

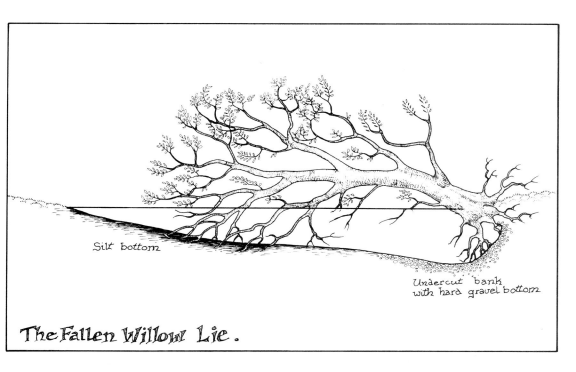

Silt bottom

Undercut bank
with hard gravel bottom

The Fallen Willow Lie.

The river flows on, growing all the while, into the forbidden Bayfield Estate with its fine hall and trees and stone bridges over the rushing water. And then it leaves for its last two miles to the village of Cley and the sluices and the marsh where it noses its way into the salt.

During these mellow summer evenings the whole Glaven valley lies still. There is not a breeze over the patchwork of fields, no clouds moving in the dimming sky. The trails of smoke from the cottages rise straight and disappear. The sun lies on the hills and in the infinite velvet sky sometimes floats a plane, its sound lost it flies so high. For a moment the brightness from the West catches it. It looks still and bright as a star.

It was on such an evening that I had on my best fish from the Glaven this summer, at Savory's Bend, a mile upstream of the sluice, just before the poplar wood.

Savory's Bend, because, of course, the river loops on Mr Savory's land, the rich flood meadow of which he is so fond. On several days I met him, following the dyke to the bend where the fallen willow lies, his rod made up, ready for a cast or two. He is old enough not to give a damn if he catches or not, simply pleased to be fishing when the weather is warm and shafts of sun glint on the water. His cane rod is a part of him, grafted to him, as though a gnarled, aged tree has grown one peculiarly straight branch. So too his fishing hat, that has been with him so often, has contracted or expanded so snugly that not a midge can get inside, or a breeze underneath. A retired legal man, a gentleman, who fishes in a suit, always wears a tie and never goes out with even the ghost of a stubble on his chin.

The crutched willow is the key to the Bend, a big white willow over thirty feet high, that caught the eye of a night storm and toppled into the river. It was saved from total collapse by the two immense branches that plunged into the sand and gravel and supported the rest of the tree at a rough forty-five degrees. This event of a few seconds, when the winter had never been blacker and the gale held sleet in it, created a classic lie for a big fish.

The tree lived on in its new position and each year the tangle of water skirting branches shoot, grow leaves, harbour insects and provide an umbrella of shade and a shield of impenetrable security. All this alone would ensure fish, but I found that another happy chance had occurred. The willow had been growing half in the river and half in the bankside so that, as it fell, the roots tore out and upwards, leaving a huge vacuum behind them, instantly filled with the rush of water. The cavern that had been created is now the centre of the lie where I found the biggest fish hide in the heat, moving out only as the evening slips into night.

This summer when I visited it, the lie was hardly ever disturbed. The far bank is unfished, and is so wild now, it is unfishable. Long grasses, meadowsweet, marsh marigolds and buttercups overhang the water and shed a stream of insects and grubs that are carried into the willow branches downstream. From the near bank fishermen are rarely deadly, breezes and currents make it impossible to put a fly in close enough. A few small browns can be picked up from the fringes of the tree but the heart of the lie is left impregnable.

On one night, though, I was successful, nearly. Beyond my dreams, almost.

★   ★   ★

Two miles below Savory's Bend the tide and the evening happened to coincide. Out from the shingle wall of the beach, the water lost its brilliant daytime blue and something moved there. Something had sensed the falling light and smelled the turn of the currents once more. Still as oil, the water had begun to press over the warm sandbars of the estuary mouth. At the Cley sluices, the Glaven was slowing as it met the turbid salt water, churning up the channel towards it. In the dykes of the marsh, the fishing boats rose and pulled against their moorings, and green crabs slunk from their stone and piling homes. Yet, the big fish was still a shadow.

I can only guess when the fish nosed into the estuary and slid

through the sluices into the fresh water. Perhaps at the head of the tide, a little after midnight, she set on the course that had to lead her to the willow. Surely at dawn, as the first lights danced off the mists, she found herself on the bend where, like any night creature, she looked for sanctuary. Into the cavern, through the willow roots, she went to stay out the day. This is where I saw her in the early morning, as I walked the west bank, before breakfast.

I had climbed the trunk of the leaning willow tree and looked through the branches into the shaded waters that ran four or five feet deep over a sand and gravel bottom. The lie was bare of weed but for strands of water buttercup on the fringe of the tree where light could penetrate. Among them, two good brown trout lay, alert, fanning the current, feeding in a casual way.

But, where the bed slid away into the void under the roots, lay the fish, bright as a fallen star, ice sparkling as a Nordic princess. Only a few hours in fresh water, her sea salt silver scales had not dimmed. She was a new run fish. A sea trout, and a big one. She was not feeding, not moving, a lost spirit in the daytime.

Over and over, I climbed to watch her, beneath me, still as an effigy on a marble tomb, frozen into a world of her own. Hers was a mind cut off from the sunlight, the dippers, the bird-song: she waited for dusk and the moon to move once more. Throughout, I wondered if she would feed then, and if she did, whether she would stray far enough from the branches to be covered. At seven, on a mild clear evening, I left for the river again.

Upstream I went, heading for the poplar wood and the best of the evening rise, for the willow on the bend and my fish. The evening was warm, humid almost, with midges everywhere and twilight birds amongst them. It was a perfect night to be out and I felt the perfection too, of walking with a wand of a rod and a box of flies that weighed no more than a crop of thistle-down.

I crossed the dyke, upped the style and entered upon Mr Savory's meadow. Just beneath the willow, by the groyne, was the man himself, surrounded by browns well into their rise. I edged past and settled upstream, in the loosestrife, opposite the willow.

[40]

For an hour, till the sun had set and gone, the rise was continuous and frantic, but I simply waited and he did not prick a fish. We conferred. Yes, he had put on a Black Gnat, and yes, of course, he had switched to an Iron Blue, and then searched his box for his smallest Grey Duster. We agreed that neither of us had anything tiny enough to imitate the reed smuts on the water and in my hair and he left whilst the twilight was bright enough for me to watch him to his car.

Then I was quite alone. The owls called. Whilst the moon was still paper thin above, mist began to form in the lows of the marshes. Under the willow, the two good browns became increasingly active, coming right to the fringe of the tree so that I almost risked a cast to them. But, somehow, the welling of the water, the heaviness of some of the ripples convinced me to stay my rod.

Moths appeared on the river, skating like confetti cast away. Within the willow a broad black neb reached for one, then another and I saw that the sea trout could, with luck, be mine. I waited, watching long enough to know exactly where she lay, then tied on a large pale sedge and began to make the nightmarish cast, behind over the nettles and grasses, and forwards until the fly almost brushed on the silver-fish leaves of the willow.

The cast travelled on a prayer and the sedge landed two feet upstream of the last of the ripples. Nothing else in life existed for me. The twenty-four inch drift became an ocean in time, until the nose came up again and the mouth engulfed me with a moist kiss. A coil of line tightened around my fingers and she was on her way.

She leapt seven times, and I left the bend bound for the sluices in her wake. She led me over the stile and down the straight. I fought her a while but the devil in her took me downriver again towards the bridge. By then it was night. The buttress blocked me. I could go no further, could do nothing more than dig in there to fight it out. Under the arches, her tail beat the water and what moon there was played on her flanks as she twisted. And then, just when hope was rising in me that I could tame her, there was nothing but twenty yards of slack line trailing in the flow.

[41]

Not for the last time this summer did my dreams melt, vanish without trace, like overwintered snows in the springtime. Nowhere does disappointment strike so hard and so quickly as in fishing, where the divide between triumph and desolation is the hair's breadth of a three pound line or the hold of a tiny hook.

But again, that night on the Glaven, I had already had my sport. I would not have killed the fish, but only nursed her well again under the moonlight, as I did with a big trout on my next river, the Bure. The art of fly fishing lies in deceiving the fish and in playing it, not in being the fishmonger, and I consoled myself with that fact as I left the Glaven for new experiences.

The Bure

Rain, a lot, a little, any rain. The Norfolk countryside cried out
for it. Rain had not fallen for weeks. Clouds had massed, come
overhead and gone. Thunder had crackled, lightning had struck
but the air remained dry. The land was parched, dried as hard as a
clay pot. The crops were wilting. The village pond deserted its
ducks. The cottagers watered their borders every evening, talking over the hedges as they did so, until the harvest flies and
midges became too bad and forced them indoors for the night.

In their bedrooms, the heat of the day remained. The pantile
roofs stored up the sun's rays and baked like ovens into the attics
beneath. It was like sleeping in a gentle stove and only for a while
before dawn was there any cool. Few could have slept under
covers and, a little after sunrise, it was warm once more.

Men harvesting day long, sweated in the dust of the combines
or the potato fields. Machinery overheated. Horseflies were
everywhere, both in shade and full sunlight. And, worst of all,
the summer day seemed interminably long, from eight in the
morning to the same hour at night.

How slowly the sun seemed to roll through the sky and drop
to rest. How they dreamed of the village pub at the crossroads,
with the cold tile floors and dark, cool tap room. It was here that I
met R., the River Keeper, on the day that he said he would show
me the Bure.

We began our trek of the valley when the heat was at its most
intense, a little after two in the afternoon. Along the lane the dust
billowed as we walked. A path led down to the river, we crossed
by a plank bridge and found the anglers' way through the hay

[43]

meadows. On the slow sloping valley sides waved the corn and
at times we passed through woods of oak, stands of poplar, a
hamlet of estate cottages and two farmyards. There was a white
Norfolk mill midway and bridges here and there. I had the
impression of a time-forgotten, lovely place, but in real truth, I
was oblivious to it all, dizzying in the heat and lost in wonder for
the river. The River Keeper became a latter-day Merlin for those
few hours, journeying from magic into miracle.

In actual fact, the man is a conjuror. Until a few years back the
lower water was a roach river, but, with belief and hard work, it
has been made fit for trout. More than that, as the tour progres-
sed, I realised that it has become a palace for them. He knows the
habitats of fish and what trout want in a river to make them stay,
overwinter and grow into big fish.

So, R. designed the lies I saw that afternoon. Groynes were

built to push the water along faster, to encourage the current to shift off the accumulated silt and expose the gravel and chalk runs for insects to colonise. Fast water weed was introduced both to promote insect life and to give the trout the shade that they seek in the brightness of the day. Trees, alder and willow especially, were planted to give more shelter, to provide the fall of terrestrial titbits onto the water, to create for some fish a secure home within the submerged roots, and to help camouflage the careful fisherman. The cow drink had been waded and rewaded, dragged and raked and kicked about until the mud and muck of ages lifted off and rolled away in the current to leave the sand and shingle I saw shine that summer's day.

R. had loaded flints and large stones into shallow runs, to break the flow, create a good oxygenating ripple, shelter for more insects and also crayfish, bullheads and loach – all food for bigger trout. Brown trout lay here and there, in the pockets behind the rocks and sometimes in front of them, where the current deflected in two around them. They were saturated in light and oxygen, in currents and counter currents, in a playground of whirlpools and eddies.

By the later afternoon, we reached the lower of the two beats, where the valley widened out a little and the crops stretched from horizon to horizon. We were in the estate of D.C., who had been the river's benefactor, who had been central to the whole project, who was the best type of landowner in the tradition of the great Norfolk gentry, the Cokes, the Townsends and the Walpoles. That day I was in the lands of more than a farmer, of a man who works so that everything in his control is developed to its limits. The general rape of the countryside is halted on his estates: I saw trimmed hedgerows, not the featureless expanses where they had been rooted out. His gates are well hung and the posts creosoted and new stands of woodland, R. says, appear every year. He takes time over his carp ponds as well as his pheasants and partridges and he cared enough to see his stretch of water as fine a river as it could possibly become.

Evening was in when R. and I parted, at a bridge over the river. Shadows were falling like dead men into the infinite peace

[45]

around. Whilst the light still gave I watched a trout beneath me, upstream of the parapet on a broad shallows. To hold position there his tail beat over a hundred times every minute, every hour of every day that he survived through the season. Over ten minutes, he rose six times, to kiss a fly from precisely the same window above his head.

I turned to look downstream, into the deep pool below the bridge, overhung by willow and by now well into dusk. Good sized fish moved lower down, on the tail, but three times small fish sprinkled onto the surface and a vortex swirled beneath them, so violent that the wake from it lifted the bankside cress. I stayed alone, well into darkness, then left to plan for, and later still to dream of, the coming day on the river, with Reelscreamer, my old companion.

★   ★   ★

Reelscreamer was by the bridge, watching the river. He was set in a world of blue and green.

The weed fanning over the gravel was a carpet of green, the bottle-green of the ranunculus and the hallucination lime green of the shell-shaped starwort clumps: the poplars alternated grey and then turquoise green and the wind combed their leaves: the oaks were heavy green, like the watercress beds, and the green of the white willows was a silver tinted one. The banks were green, nettle and dock green, all overhanging, reflecting in the river along with the blue of the sky.

The meadow grass was thick, spangled in a heavy dew that did not clear till late morning. There was mist along the dykes, where the lapwings called, sometimes in haze, sometimes in sunshine. Already a combine was at work, just off the plain.

The cool of the early morning had brought more trout into open water than I had seen the afternoon before. They looked golden, or perhaps amber, as though they attracted the sun's rays to them and glowed like living coals or darting arrows of fire. Excitement was on us both, the thrill that cannot be denied when

a fisherman, his trout and the river are all in harmony and perfect unison. We hurried our different ways leaving footprints in the dew.

We had two hours of fishing before us. We knew that the cool of the morning is fragile, soon lost and, when the heat of the day arrived, it did so irresistibly. As the sun rose it shimmered bright enough to drain the mists and bleach the lights and colours from the day. It baked the valley, filled it with the drone of warm air flies and drove the cattle off the plain to lie in the ditches and the thorn tree scrubs. Not even the cool water of the spring-fed river could save our fishing beyond late morning.

I had begun by watching from behind a two trunk willow tree the trout on the thin water of a cattle drink. They were feeding fish, flashing flank to the gravel, harrying the shrimps and nymphs amongst the stones. I stalked them patiently, like a heron, but only raised four lances of water that fled into the dense weed beds above. Even a No. 5 line whispered out through the rings, landed like a telegraph wire in that unforgiving light.

Reelscreamer was already back by the bridge, one trout on the grass beside him, where he lay pub dreaming with the pool at his feet. We sat there awhile, slightly in the shade from the overhead sun, silent by the deep water that could provide anonymity for any fish however large.

The pool asleep in the day, opaque, green, now grey but always with a shade of blue overall, was like a misted window pane only hinting at what lay on the other side. Neither of us could see the bed of the river, but monsters rose out of the guesses.

Church bells were ringing. The morning had gone, gulped away by the endless fascination, the consuming concentration of river trouting, and though Reelscreamer had to leave, I decided to return at dusk, at that hour when a big fish had fed in the pool the night before. There was a run between shallows and drop off, where the water deepened over large stones before falling into the pool itself. I waded in and overturned some of the flints and half bricks there. Crayfish, bullheads, loaches, nymphs, caddis, snails and an infestation of shrimps fled into the silt puffs. That was where I would put my fly, come the dusk.

So, Reelscreamer left me; back to city life. I returned to the river at eight. It was warm still. The wind had died and hardly a breath stirred the poplars. At the tail of the pool, well beneath the willow a fish was rising steadily and, as half-light and the big fish were over an hour away, I decided to try him. As well as I can present a fly, I put six different dry ones to him and failed utterly. Perhaps it was the watercress. Here it encroached out from both banks creating a narrow, fast-flowing middle channel. Either I avoided catching the cress and threw too straight a line that immediately dragged, or I landed in the cress which pulled the fly off course within two feet of its run. A clever summer trout would not be deceived.

Now the time drew on to that moment when the high summer day had become dusk, when I could not see a dry fly at five yards, when the swallows had given the air over totally to the bats and when once more big fish moved on the head of the pool, just out from the dark skirts of the willow tree. Moths showered like snowflakes. The silence was intense, then a bat fluttered on leather wings, a chaos of cricket legs built up in the long grasses and a screech owl cried in the poplars.

The rises became heavy. A constant rippling of water lifted the cresses as though the pulse of the river were racing harder. The whole valley had shrunk down onto me and this one lie, and I looked up to escape from the closeness of it all, to still my heart and steady my casting wrist. There were a million stars out that I felt I could reach more easily than the fish in the universe beneath me.

Trout moved onto the stony water I had explored earlier. Small fish were being harried once more. I cast four yards upstream, a mere flick to where the shadow of the bridge cut across what glow remained of the sunset. The shrimp, lightly leaded, landed with a sound only slightly above the burble of the nightjar. I strained to see its course and could not. I tried to sense its fall and to keep contact with it, coming back towards me. I believed I could feel it catch at stones. It had to be going through fish. Were they seeing it? Were they following it? A bat caught

[49]

the fly line and I smothered a strike. I worked the shrimp a little faster than the river and inched it from the bottom. The take came as an explosion of sight and sense that hit my eye and arm together and for five minutes my brain and body worked through the whirlwind of a big fish, on a tight line in the near darkness. Only when I had beaten him could I make a conscious decision, to return him.

The hook slid free where he lay, in the watercress at my feet. His breath came back once more in sobs that blew bubbles through his gills, onto the shallows and away downstream. His body righted and in that instant of movement caught the gleam of a winking, watching star. I left the Bure as I found it.

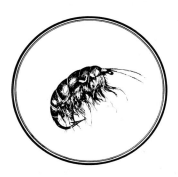

THE SOUTH

Southern Chalk Streams

When it is dark early, and the wind has bite, then imagine writers at their desks. The fishing is done and now they cast their tales in the flickers of fire and lamplight. Good writers and great fishermen all embedded in their sport, all struggling with the one eternal impossibility: describing the invisibility of the waters of the chalk streams, waters that have no more colour, taste or smell than the air itself.

They try 'gin clear' and then 'crystal clear', squint at the descriptions through the shadow and cross them out. 'Pellucid' sounds better. Perhaps the trout could be 'transparent', or like 'fish in a goldfish bowl' but these words are all short of the magic in the mind's eye.

What so many writers have tried to do is essential to their works. They feel a compulsion to show how a trout lies in a world so pure, so radiant, so afire with ice light that every fin's ray, fleck and scale is washed and polished by this glittering water until it shines. They need to tell how this chalk water is transformed, somehow conjured into airy nothingness, how the weed furls and unfurls like a lace curtain on a light breeze, how the pondskater hangs like a spider on his web and how a trout hovers as magically as a humming-bird.

Perhaps the writer gets up and stalks the room, frustrated at the knot that he cannot cut, angry with the dead, dull page he has written, so far from the light dancing stream he loves and grasps out for. It becomes an obsession to produce one paragraph of enchantment because it is the wondrous invisibility of his chalk water that makes all his trout fishing so total an experience. It is this curious fact that the water does not screen or separate him from his quarry that is so important. All through a summer's day, at least until the shadows fall, the river is no barrier to him at all. Often the water is only apparent as an element at all, because the current crinkles it, a coot splashes it in defiance, or best of all, because a trout dimples it with a kissing rise.

The writer knows that this intimacy is a blessed charge: he and his fish are so close, so thinly separated by a gossamer film, that they could be existing in the same element. He knows his trout, and it is as though they know him. He can fish with absolute discrimination, try for just one fish and if he fails he can pursue it next day, next week, next season or in his next dream.

So, you see how in this way chalk stream trout become immortalised. They are beautiful, easily recognised and annual companions. The southern chalk stream maestros have moved from the realm of ordinary fishing into a new world, a dimension only a few know. And the trout that they pursue similarly become famous for eternity.

Witness the poem of Patrick Chalmers, 'To an Old Friend', the trout still swimming below his weir as the season fell upon them both. The sadness in it is not because the fish has not been caught, but because the special relationship may not be renewed, the trout may not ever be there again, but hopefully . . .

> may Easter find us at the trysting place,
> There where the dancing bubbles spin and race,
> To meet the first March Brown.

Howard Marshall knew such a chalk stream friend, Sammy — four pound monster of the Lambourn. And there was three pound Henry caught from one of Douglas McCraith's 'Dancing Streams'.

I myself possess such a fish, though the glory is very much second hand. It is a Kennet trout, caught in 1879 weighing five and a quarter pounds. It was set up by Taxidermist Cooper, and I came by it many years ago. There is a faded fly in the case, a type of mayfly, I think, which would fit the date plate — the first of

June, in those last months of Disraeli's ministry. The gut is still there, and the knot, and I would not now trust either on a gudgeon and I reckon even then the fish was landed by a whisker, on a prayer . . .

Minutes passed before he broke surface, where his mouth was held clear for an instant, perhaps two. A gulp of air got into him and he had trouble in sounding. Next time he came up more easily and a second and a third gasp of oxygen flooded the channels of his body. Now, he could not get half down. His stability was gone. His belly flashed as he slowly revolved in weed and water as the fight and the might drained away. The will of this great fish had gone and after all those years, the rush of mayfly blood had conquered him.

No equipment in the nineteenth century less than a salmon net could easily cope with the twenty-one inch fish, but the angler made do and the fish now above me, was banked. The angler was trembling. The fish was dying and the reign of the King of the Kennet Willows was over.

A telegraph was sent to Radnor Street. The corpse was sent by the night train and next day a boy was despatched from St Lukes to collect it. Cooper had only been in business for nine years. This was an important commission, there were rivals for it so he needed to get it right: that vision of invisible water, of the fish hanging like a humming-bird was in his head, and again we see an artist attempting to re-create impossibility.

So, imagine once more a man with a problem, resurrecting, physically, a dead trout. A fish whose skin had parched and wrinkled, whose cream belly and crimson splashed flanks had glazed into uniform dullness, whose eye was sunk and blank now, whose fins were curled and split and whose entire body had slumped into shapelessness – this trout Cooper had to re-create as a vibrant creature, risen like magic from the Radnor Street workshop.

He succeeded as well as any craftsman might, who is not Lord of Creation himself. His work still has something of grace about it and something still of power around the hunched shoulders. And when the firelight catches and flashes in the eye, for an

instant you could imagine it was again the June sunlight twink-
ling there as the giant made his last, fatal rise a century and five
years ago.

Reelscreamer's Letter

Reelscreamer you have met on the Bure. He is the greatest friend and a good fisherman, which is better than a good friend and the greatest fisherman. As a fisherman he does have faults. His casting could be better, he does get into tangles whatever the wind speed, then always complains about bad keepering, and he does play a fish very heartily indeed, hence his name. But as a friend he is faultless. He is generous with everything he owns, knowledge and possessions. He is amusing. He drinks very enthusiastically and, above all, he is quick to include me on the best beats of his life.

This year he was lucky enough to get one of these rare gems on the Nadder and the letter was fast in coming. The core of it I reproduce. It gives the spirit of the man. It shows why many men fish. It sheds a personal light on the charm of a chalk stream day. It really is Reelscreamer let loose on thick writing paper, with a gin, I suspect, to his hand.

Dear John,

Please come down soon whilst the mayfly are about and even I can catch the odd fish. Or failing that, visit later in the summer when I get really stuck and look at the patterns in the fly box with that despair that overtakes me when there are fish around and I haven't the faintest notion where to start. (If only Plato had been a fisherman in the way that all fishermen are philosophers perhaps he would have found that paradigm of flies that I seek – just think of it, 'Plato's Paradigm'; it has a sort of ring about it, don't you think?)

The journey itself is rich enough, along a soft Wiltshire valley, corn golden now on the angel downs and a kestrel holding the air over the ancient tumulus. Best of all is the crumbling barn, right down by the river, that you can just see from the road. Soft handmade bricks, slipped tiles and rotting doors to the grain store on the first floor. A couple of times I've turned the MG off down the lane to it and mused: that would be the life – a porch with a cane rod made up behind the door, an attic window overlooking the stream's course, summer and winter, a vice at the desk ready to copy the flies the moment they lift off the water that flows by the lawn, preparing a light green English salad from the garden and then a relaxed hour at last light to take a couple of browns about a pound and a bit each, and a glass or two of white wine. You've heard this stuff of dreams before, but the place is as they say 'ripe for modernisation'.

The river is little fished but there are some sentry posts – picket points are a better description this summer – where men have stood and fished. You know the places. The crushed grass and bruised nettles where the skim of soil begins to show through the moss. Each week I try to work out the strategy behind them all. What fish are these stations in the reed covering? Or, I know you are into this at the moment, are they placed for the lies only the old river hands know about? Or is it only because behind them there are no trees and banks to trap the back cast? Or is it because all 'once a week fishermen' herd to the same places as a bolster to their confidence? Anyway, I await your reaction and explanation.

The river here is pretty nearly like that which flowed out of Eden, at least the seeds from it have blown here. But there are problems. There is the Creeping Beat Cheater, a common plague down here, apparently. The C.B.C. is on beat number four. My beat is upstream and each week I will be half-way up when he appears at the bottom marker willow, trespasses a hundred yards and then I wave and he scuttles off. I wave because I feel that we could exchange beats for the day. I put down my gear, throw off my jacket and set off after him with the offer. He retreats so quickly, I feel a fool and stop, but after an hour he returns and the game continues. One of these weeks, on our mutual glory day, I have decided to climb up the willow and wait for him, perhaps dressed as an owl!

C.B.C. is a small headache compared with the fish themselves. I have one day a week. Perhaps the weed has been cut and is coming down in rafts, or perhaps there is a cold wind, or a mist, or it rains all day. And yet I am supposed to be able to identify flies and feeding habits. How am I ever going to distinguish one upwinged fly from another without telescopes strapped to my eye sockets? Sometimes when I drive home, I feel the books are written from one expert to another with hardly a thought to the average angler. You fish every day of the week. Remember, as you write this book, that you are pretty nearly alone in that.

There is a bit too much weed on the river now, for my liking. In certain lights that water buttercup looks like stubble on a man's chin. It spoils the look for me. It spoils the fishing. It is like the mole on my cheek that I have to avoid when I am shaving. If I don't avoid the mole I get cut, and I can't avoid the weed and get hung up. I know you will creep and crawl and drool over some weeded up lie it would need a magician to cover, but I would like to see it out. That is how we suburban anglers are, on eight hours fishing a week.

My beat has a cowdrink on it and they mean as much to me as lies do to you. The one here is a good one. Heavy imprints here, shallow sand there and it is a really finely mottled example. The barbed wire fence though, is a classic. You know all drinks are wired off to stop the stupid beasts going too far – well, here it is single strand, buried in the silt in five places at least. Best of all, not one of the fence posts is straight. Four are askew, two have fallen over and I suspect some more have washed away. And, of course, there is always a prime fish lying just behind the last post and many of my best flies are attached to the wire. A bizarre version of a gamekeeper's larder, if you like, but nymphs and Greenwells instead of magpies and jays! It is a triumph of agricultural architecture, beautiful in any light and speaks for all country kind in its slapdash way. Spick and span in town and make do if you can is countryside and my cowdrink.

A chalk river is very quiet and if you are dreaming, the splash of a fish startles you. I will stand there in the Nadder Valley and cock an ear and hardly hear a sound. Then, perhaps a plane, the wind lifting the leaves a little, a woodpecker or a jay, but as a man I feel alone. And then the valley can be strange, almost frightening.

Perhaps it is the murmur of the storms that follow it, the rain smoking off the trees, or the burial mounds atop the hills – but when the low clouds mask the sun, you feel a twentieth century intruder, for an instant rocked into the past whilst the true hunter turns in his thunderstruck barrow.

Not so in Celtic rivers where the bubble of free water laughs over all sounds. I have never felt apprehension there – they flow through the ribs and sinews of ancient rocks not old peoples . . .

The letter continued and the excitement he felt reached me and I knew long before its end that I would be on my way South as soon as I could settle my affairs.

The Nadder

I left Norfolk very early in the morning, only just after midnight really, for the long drive southwards, through the lonely Suffolk Chases across half a dozen counties into Wiltshire. Occasional juggernauts rumbled past, shaking the night as they went. Small towns, villages, roadside hamlets were all dark and locked up tight. Only cats and a single urban fox were on the move. Owls in the headlights, and pigeons pecking on the road grit as the light grew. 4.30 a.m. Dawn is a trace in the East, a crack separating the rim of the earth and the dome of the sky. Air from the open window keeps me awake. Familiar smells of summer linger, a whiff of burnt straw, the sweet smell of all-night pea viners, a dampness of a clear sky dew. Closing now, in the real South, where there is a blueness over the downs, and the stars flicker and fade as the lemon lights of the new day strike them. The cruel pike's tooth moon hangs there longer, loses its shine. I am in a ribbon of mist. The Nadder Valley.

Reelscreamer is asleep at the wheel of his car. His tousled head takes a time to clear and then smiles a big welcome. We stretch against the parapets of the bridge. An early trout is already rising, in a nonchalant way; another hot day.

The big man headed the MG off the lane on to a track; and what good fishing water is not down a track that digs and delves into its own unique wonderland? All mystery, all smell of woodland and bracken, all noisy with jays, with scrabbling rabbits and croaking toads lured out by the dew. Owners of the forest, big eyed at the tyres munching on the brick rubble, at the groaning chassis that works like a ship in a storm over the ruts and tractor marks. The first sight of the water now, first smell of water mint, of loosestrife, sound of the first rise on the straight – there, there again.

I do love tracks.

That particular fish I got close to at once. I was allowed guest's rights. I made him out above the weed, just on the crease between current and slack, about a foot down, a good brown, under the shade of alder branches. Hardly working to hold position, intercepting food just now and again, a fish enduring a hot weather feeding rhythm, that breaks surface in a languid way. And if he missed the fly, by design or carelessness (who could tell which?), he never made a second attempt. An uncaring fish. He was little concerned if he bit lucky or not.

When he did catch, then he chewed slowly, thoughtfully. Every vein of every wing, every last antenna was considered and even in swallowing, the trout took his time. He bellowed and flared his gills, just as though even then with the meal in his gullet, he could not decide whether to reject or ingest. And when all was done, then his eye rolled round once or twice, and then perhaps again before he shook himself into a leisurely activity once more. You know when you have seen a trout that is unlikely to make mistakes.

The bank where we were was planted with immense white willows. Southern willows have a grace you do not see elsewhere in England. The colours have more variance, their size is greater, they grow into temples of trees that weep and flow in the breezes. Perhaps in these mild valleys the winds are not too severe, or the softer winters let them grow longer into the autumn, stir earlier in the spring, and live to older ages. Perhaps the soil is richer, pumps more life and moisture into them and brings them on to this luxuriant beauty.

I sat against one, the giant of them all, thick boled, tattooed with deep grain, that cast a shade over the water, not darkening it as much as shielding it from glare. I was in a light that was lime green, shot sometimes with brighter arrows of sunlight. I simply watched the river.

There were no trout on the top, nor in mid water. Below me

[62]

the Nadder ran five feet deep over fine, bright gravel ribbed with weed, and it was here I saw the trout. Several fish were browsing, acting like a shoal of coarse fish, standing on their heads, rooting in the thin silt, even sucking in pebbles in their food search. These were not lie fish, intercepting and ambushing food. They were working for food in a steady, systematic way. When they disappeared out of sight, under the trailing fingers of willow, I had no suspicion their behaviour changed. Any fly that I or Reelscreamer put in their paths would be at least three feet above their heads, unless it were heavily weighted and fished very slow. And that shook me no end.

Upstream of me, the water plunged away down, black with a great depth. A stray limb of the willow clawed beneath the surface, snatched at the passing debris and built up an immense raft of soft weed. Between its edge, and the bank, and the willow was a triangle of clear water and I peered in.

There were fry shoals working in the upper layers, and young dace beneath them, but under them was a head of ominous size. Its body was in the willow roots, only its head could you see. It was not a pike, there was none of that shovel headed flatness. It could not have been a barbel hanging in mid water – even if there are any in the Nadder – but it could have been a chub. There was something blunt headed about it, but it still lacked the bulbous eyes and the big flared nostrils, not to mention the coarse slobber lipped mouth. I hardly dared think of it as a trout, because by that skull it was a five pounder and I shake when big fish are about.

It was the perfect lie; food came to it from the raft, dropping as the weed came to rest. And not an angler a month would see the fish or guess at its existence. Hot days would not trouble him there in the gloom, he need only travel at dusk if he still needed food. So perfect was his fortress, I could not even dap a shrimp to him with any hope of success.

★   ★   ★

A warmth to melt butter, a day becalmed in the rays of the sun. The trout were in the weed for good till dusk. Only a phenomenon could have brought them out.

Now such a thing did not happen, but half a stroke of luck came my way, even if I mistook it for the kiss of death at the time. Someone, somewhere, on this my golden day was cutting weed and great mats of the stuff were coming our way. I simply wandered off upstream, rod very limply held in hand.

After quarter of a mile the river came out of a thick woodland belt, with a hay meadow opposite it. At one point two oaks grew out low across the stream forming an umbrella across the river's width, throwing a canopy of dapple and shade. Right where the furthest oak skimmed the water, a trout was working quite busily. There was no apparent pattern to his activity that I could see, but it was quite a spree. Watery kisses on the top he would follow with gentle head and tail porpoise takes, swirling under the surface and even flashing deep down, intercepting items nearly past him. Only when he rammed the latest floating jungle, when his jaw appeared right through it to steal some shrimp, did I realise he was eating indiscriminately at anything the drift brought him. Anything that I presented realistically might be taken, if I did not scare him, and if he spotted it amongst the debris.

I discounted a dry fly: the line would be bound to catch the rafts and cause drag. And I doubted if it would be picked out amongst the surface filth. I fancied something just sub-surface, but again I realised I would never see the leader move in amongst the debris. So, it was to be a leaded Olive Nymph, then, that would hit with a plop, be taken or rejected at once, and, if taken, hit hard.

To present that nymph, though, was no such theoretical exercise. There was ranunculus on either side of the trout, branches all over his heavens, and the blankets of weed were growing in size and number. In thirty minutes, I put out five failed attempts. The old cane rod was perhaps too soft and slow to put down a nymph fast, but it was a good length and even if a cast failed, at least it slapped onto the weed, never rippling the water or disturbing the fish.

Perhaps it was a brainwave, or was it a cheat, but I went fifty yards upstream of that top oak and with a long branch diverted a dozen rafts in towards the bank to let them trundle down the margin. Looping back to my rod, exactly a minute after I returned, twenty clear yards of water approached. After ten had gone over, I made one careful cast.

Reelscreamer was with me by then, and netted it deftly, but it was a fight that made the ferrules groan, the sound that became my yardstick of a fish's power that summer.

After it, we returned downstream together and sat on a wooden bridge, watching the river beneath. My heart still beat loud, there was a tightness in the temples, and my hands shook: a trout on a fly from a chalk stream on a hot cloudless day. Not that I am proud; more amazed, like a child, and that is what catching a fish like this does to me. No matter how many times a lightning trout strikes, I cannot really believe it. Such a success is so audacious that I can only put it down to a fluke, and then when it happens again, I am even more stupified and even more excited.

This is my closest bond with Reelscreamer. He enjoys catching a fish more than any man I know. It is a miracle of which he will never tire, and as a result he will never tire of life whilst there is a fish in a river anywhere.

Somewhere in the Kennet Valley

I have been puzzling a long time why it should be that this chapter means a lot to me. I have wondered if it is because the action took place on the water of a friend, or if it is down to the satisfaction I felt over the success of an unusual fly.

Perhaps I am pleased with the overall project, an idea that began in the depth of winter and was finally laid to rest in high summer. Or was it the fish on the bank – those untouched grayling, perfect as newborns – that fire me now? Probably the answer in part lies in all these things, but I am forced to decide at the end, that the whole story revolves around one small carrier pool. That tiny circumference of water, the eye of the tale, a tale that I stumbled upon during a short journey to Wiltshire.

Half lost, I was wandering on a January day when all the sedge was down, brown, withered half away, in the Kennet valley somewhere. There was a wind that turned in from the East as the hours drew on. It should have stayed there, should have left its snows over Europe. And now, here was this bleary half light valley under thick headed cloud that would not be long breaking into a storm. No birds sang.

I wandered in the meads and put up a pheasant. Its startled cries echoed and died and were not answered. The temperature fell. I knew it by the marsh muds that started to crackle beneath my boots as I went. Then it was, as a last throw, I followed a carrier from the big river. The water ran clear, very clear for the winter month, but I could not see deep for there was no light in the sky and the surface flurried and scurried in front of the ripping wind.

The willow herb was dead stalked, the poplars were bare, the afternoon drifted away from me, there seemed no point in my continuing and I was one conscious decision from returning when I found myself by the pool. I sat on the plank bridge across the hatch, watched the clouds race over the trees and the whole wood bend and sway, but the pool lay calm at my feet. It was not so much sheltered, as hidden, as secret in the fold of valley.

I could not see in, for the water turned from green, to grey, to charcoal as the twilight gathered, and I stumbled away over the plain.

In the early night, the storm blew round and round the valley and hid the world with white. Only later did the moon appear, well up, nearly full and threw a frost to hold each snow crystal tight where it lay. And when the morning dawned, it was with a frozen sun and a pitiless blue sky, and though the wind had died, the next freeze could barely wait to come to earth and hung about eagerly the day through.

Though the sun had no warmth in it, it did scrape above the tree line, and the moment its rays fell onto the valley they burned off the snow crystal and the glare became intense. Certainly now, I could see into the pool as the flood of light revealed the bed of sand and rocks and an old weed rake lying there.

Gradually, I began to imagine that I saw fish, or tricks of the light, or dead weed still rooted there, an algaed pipe or some other deceiver; but the more I looked, the more I saw and the more convinced I became that three good fish lay there before the bridge. And when one moved across the current, and another moved up against it I wondered how I had ever doubted.

Around noon the fish became very active and left the bottom and rose into mid water, higher still and even turned at times on the surface itself. I do not think I was disappointed the fish were grayling. That they were wild fish and not stocked only added to the intimacy of the pool. And, after all, they were big grayling.

That is how those fish in that pool set themselves in my mind for the next six months. I thought back to them often. And if I ever were near to forgetting them my memory would be jogged:

the chapter of a book that told how the great Frank Sawyer had struggled in 1958 to catch a grayling from the parent river of that carrier of mine; the trip to the border town tackle shop, where the owner told me quite unprompted, that he had tied a grayling killer, an adaptation of the Francis Francis bug. I bought several ready for the time that I would return.

★   ★   ★

Now, it was summer and the frost-blasted nettles were back tall and green, and the willow herb clustered over all the paths, and the trees were leaved out and hid landmarks I looked for. The marshes were wet and yielding again, the wind was again from the East, but now warm and happy, skipping insects and seeds up the carrier. The pool was smaller now, grown over with rushes, flag and iris. The willows pressed close round its edge gave little room to cast with the two piece that I had along with me. The water itself was lower and though not clearer – that would have been impossible – it was brighter and streaked with weed.

I lay again on the bridge at the head of the pool and began a slow methodical search through the panes of water where the current momentarily flattened out a space. A few small grayling hung around the shallows. A bullhead scampered from a rock to the weed rake and dug himself in with his frying pan pectorals. Two good browns patrolled the flow from the hatch, very busy, not letting much pass. Otherwise, the open water was quite bare. I watched the weed beds. It seemed to me that in a length of ranunculus there were fronds which did not move in proper unison and river rhythm; and when a particular forceful rush of water came and lifted the entire growth, exposed there lay the three fish I so wanted to tangle with.

It was late in the day when one of the grayling began to feed. He edged out onto the gravel and began to eat hard, tipped up on his head just like a tench. He never left the bottom, but sucked and dug and stirred up silt, and shrimps and nymphs too. Quite obvious to me was the purpose of the great dorsal fin of the fish,

[70]

unfurled now in the flow. Wherever the fish moved, it was the sail above it that steered and guided and maintained the balance. Whilst the ripple through the body and the kick from the tail gave it power, the dorsal was the vital rudder. Only when the fish drifted away across the current, was it momentarily dropped, or at least lowered some.

I compared the grayling with the trout. The trout, it seemed, worked harder with all their fins and body to hold position in the current. The grayling got by more on the strength of that one expanse of bone and tissue, as large as a perch's, but more supple – a dorsal fin for all purposes.

As I slipped into position, I knew any fly must sink fast, to plummet past the trout and reach the grayling as quickly as possible. I knew the fly I chose must also hold bottom well, for that was where, exclusively, the grayling was feeding. And I knew that I must be close enough to see the fly itself, for the grayling's mouth is so small and neat that there is not the tell-tale gob of white that a trout makes at a fly.

My hands shook just a little as I tied on a pale cream killer bug, well weighted, and flexed the little old rod to loosen me up. I checked all around for snags and hang ups and let the bug go three or four yards upstream. It fell past the trout and settled in the sand. I could see it clearly.

So far so good. I began to work it towards the still burrowing grayling. Now, when it came to within about six inches, just to the left of the fish, that dorsal swung in the current and the grayling moved up very close. The bug was hidden by the fish itself. I could feel nothing through the line. I took a chance and tightened. At once the fish rolled belly up, knocked off balance, and I had him fairly and firmly by the nose.

It was no great fight, and indeed I hurried it up a fair bit because I wanted the fish to go back as little tired as possible. I never even held him, just unhooked him on the watercress, admired his slimness, his gudgeon scales, that red tinged sail fin with its heavy fleckings, the flank that turned from silver to blue to pink to pearl as the light caught it and his tiny underslung mouth. I put him around two pounds and let the water receive him.

A Lady on the Avon

The nights have drawn in. The rabbits are on the meadow by late afternoon and the breeze is cold. There are no swallows over the lake. The weed has lost its vitality and a freckling of oak leaves is on the water. The cats move from the fields as the house lights switch on and the wild deer of the wood pull clear to the farm and even shelter overnight in the long grass along the bottom boundary. The horizon looks one long stark cold sunset and soon the owls shriek. Gone are the nightingales, the nightjars and even the black rabbit.

The windows are closed and the curtains all drawn. Sounds are thrown in on themselves, a clock ticking, a coal dropping in the grate. There is no one around at night. The countryside is quiet with little journeying. The farmer, alone by the bar, is glad of someone to talk to, over a beer by the fire, before dinner and a last check on the barns, and the cattle too. He has the meadows along the river, does not fish but likes a trout. It is wetland nearly all of it, and mostly left for hay but he still keeps a careful eye overall. He certainly knows the customs of the fishermen along the four mile beat. He recognises every single one of them.

The ceiling is low above him, smoked russet brown, all wrinkled, sagging and beamed, that keeps in the heat and damps down the light. A weather rutted face his, or perhaps because he laughs a lot, and most especially at the fishermen he sees. Objects of amusement we all are. And of interest for one habit in particular, which he cannot understand: it is the way each man, every visit, goes to his own favoured length of water. There are no beat rules here. We fish by choice, guided by passion for a place, dreams of a particular fish in a particular lie. Lies we each of us believe in and hope for every visit.

He cannot possibly understand that skip of heartbeat when we find the pull-in empty for us, see no figure stalking our own piece of skyline and follow no other's tracks over the marsh to our especial copse. The farmer laughs more when I tell him about the child who gets back into every man however old, and who pushes him at the fastest he goes all week across the water meadows, urging him on over marsh and dyke, through the flag iris to that place he believes in and has planned for. To the farmer, fishing he can only understand as a lapse into relaxation, or as an excuse for idleness. He laughs even more to know that it is the exact reverse of these things. To explain, I told him about the Lady on the Avon.

★   ★   ★

A golden afternoon, hazed with heat and shimmering under a blinding sun that hardly seemed to move in the sky and that drugged everything down the valley. I had my old rod with me, still in its bag, for I had seen nothing to make me want to fish. The pools were sluggish and dead so I kept on the move, upstream, crossing the dried out ditches and skirting the outcrop of blazing white chalk.

Yard by yard, the river shallowed and ran faster, even singing again over occasional gravels. My pace slowed. I took more care how I passed the pools, until eventually, a way in the wilds, I came on an enchanted gorge, where the river ran in a series of cascades through deeply cut, willow dotted banks: the first moving creatures of the walk were active there, some splendid, busily rising trout.

I slipped down into the long grasses and began to untie the bag and slip out the rod, fingering the smooth red whipping, thinking deeply. I had got as far as screwing on the reel, loading the line through the rings and even to tying on a two pound tippet when on the bank above me a breathless lady appeared. She, too,

[74]

immediately began to assemble fishing gear and had got to approximately the stage I had halted at before she saw me, well hidden beneath her.

'Oh,' she gasped, still out of breath, obviously taken aback. 'Sorry. I didn't see you there. There was no car up there on the track and I rather thought . . .'

'No,' I replied, 'I walked upstream from the bridge.' With a reluctance pitiful to see, she began to reel the line back through the rings and away again onto the drum. I asked her what she was doing.

'It hardly matters. I always fish here and you're here first. There's a lot I can do at home.' But I would not take that. I could not really. She was a Member, and I was only a day guest and even more after such a glut of it, it would come as a relief not to have to fish one day. I finally assured her it was no hardship to lie in a sweet smelling meadow and just watch the river. She accepted, and how pleased I became, because she was to treat me to the definitive demonstration of lie fishing.

Possibly out of her experience of the pools, possibly because of inbuilt watercraft, she showed me perfect knowledge of the bankside, where to step, how to move, and how to blend into the trees and bushes that all but blotted her image out. Even treading on the gravel, the stones never rattled or moved or betrayed her in any way. Constantly aware of the sun's angle, her shadow never fell within a yard of the water: she even seemed to foretell the breezes, for her fly always seemed to land wherever there was a passing, slight ripple on the water. There she was, moving in the little gorge, fishing busily, very active and yet that awareness of her surroundings kept her totally hidden from the trout. I could see that from my high bank. They rose without a suspicion in the world even when she was almost on top of them.

She was just as sure about the trout themselves, obviously quite happy on the whereabouts of every fish along that hundred yards of prime water. She mended line exactly to suit current speeds, she cast to the bull's eye on the stickles, and picked fish out right on the line of the crease between flow and eddy. She knew the runs through the weed and steered a nymph back

through them, as though guided by some mysterious second sight. From where she crouched, she could not possibly have seen the trout beneath the underhang I had watched, but she cast onto his nose and took him.

She did it all with an unhurried action, short pin point casts that were never rushed, flustered, dropped down hard or hung up behind. She rested the lies in turn. A couple of casts to each fish and she was gone like the willow herb down that blew through her hair.

In less than two hours on what any man would have said was a hopeless day, she hooked into eight fish. And landed most. She merely tightened, never struck. Played them firm and tight, rod low, with hardly a splash. She beached them all, slipping the hook in the shallows on all but two. Then she left, thanked me and invited me to fish. And, I ask you, how could I ever follow that? As she went back to her car, the two piece remained bagged and we went home.

THE WEST

An Introduction

By the time that I arrived in the West, my respect for river trout ran high. I knew that at times I was fishing well, but often I had been forced to rely on dusk for success; or on some unexpected chance, like the weed cut on the Nadder. I had not tricked many careful fish in full daylight and I knew it. Some of the trout I had tried were all but impossible on normal gear, with straight-forward methods and plied with only average skills.

This belief grew on a journey through the South West of England, where I stopped at a hotel on a bridge by a river. I took my drink onto the lawns where the village boys were fishing into a fine lie between the stone piers of the bridge. There was a deep, dark hole, shot through with fast, swirling currents that curled around like snakes before sliding away and straightening off downstream again. There were five boys and I counted six trout.

Maggots, worms and minnows were all being used as bait, and one boy, more enterprising than the rest, had even caught a crayfish and was threading it through the line. But, despite this freedom in the rule book, action was slow. As I savoured my lager, I became aware that the capture of any trout, in any manner, was an event. Whilst they would mop up the loose fed maggots, the fish invariably left those on the hook. The minnows might be tweaked by the tail – but that was all. The worms were not even looked at. I had chanced to meet again with a common problem.

In part, the problem as I saw it, was the line. A trout has a flawless ability to see nylon of any strength. Even if you could go light enough to fool him, then you would never hold on to him.

Fish sufficiently heavy to land him and you are too clumsy to tempt him. The need for a hook does not help, either. I watched how hooked maggots sank unnaturally quickly and with restricted movements in a stiff laboured way. Similarly, minnows swam awkwardly, constricted and lopsided. The boy with the crayfish did no better. Though the hook was hidden well in the tail, the currents snatched his line and bellied it across the stream so that the little lobster was dragged up to an unusual mid water level. My nymphs and dryflies, I thought, must look absurd.

A short while later in the West, I remembered that idle hour on the sundrenched lawns. On the Wolf, the Carey and the Barle, I could never in any way forget it.

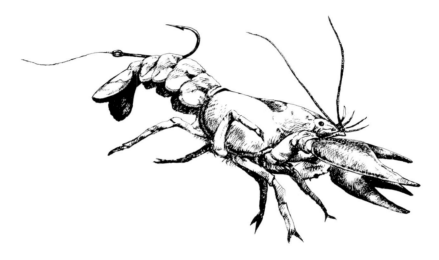

The Lyd

A man walked down the valleyside to a pool on the River Lyd, not far from its junction with the Tamar. It was a pleasant morning, only just after breakfast, and he appeared to be in no hurry. In fact, he sat looking into the water for two hours or more, content on a large rock. As the sun rose and light flooded the pool, he put on polaroid glasses and then nothing could avoid his gaze.

Eventually he moved, started to pace out lengths of bank, stood on rocks in the margins as though testing them with his weight, and finally he put up a rod and began to make casts around the pool. They were trial casts presumably, for he did not work them through properly, but looked to be preparing the way – plotting landmarks on the far bend, noting trees, boulders and underwater snags. In all, he was at the pool four hours and then he left up the steep meadow to the estate road.

All day long, the sea trout shoals lie in the river pools, never moving, sleeping princesses of the stream. Whilst in the shade, they look grey in colour, but when the sun climbs and strikes them, then they glow silver, and, realising it, they press further in under the trees, or under the slabs of stone smoothed by the centuries of flow.

There are hours of silence ahead yet in the pool before the night returns, and little will startle these lazing ladies. Disturbed, they merely stretch, lie a little lower in the water or phase away to be no more than a ripple over a sand bar, or a fleck on some rock face.

They came up the Tamar one night and turned off into the

Lyd, easing through a neck of water only six feet across with a push to it like a waterfall. So now they are tired, happy to waste away the hot fretful day with its threats of thunder. These are ladies of the night, cool and serene, with a purpose of their own hidden in the darkness.

Dusk comes all over the land after a cloud barred sunset, with sprays of stars and hushing winds, and it stirs all fish everywhere: roach in the ponds, carp in their meres, tench in the estate lakes, and eels in the ooze land dykes far away. But no other fish is so acutely a night walker as the sea trout. Only when the sun is on the horizon do they act purposefully at last. Initially it is only a quickening of their pulse, a tremor through their lovely lithe bodies. Fins that had draped, now curl on the water, feeling again; they clutch the current and warp it into patterns around them. The cooler water refreshes their gills, the softer light is more pleasant to their eyes.

One stirring fish disturbs her neighbour, who awakes in her turn, and so the awareness of the coming night spreads through them all. The shoal in the pool grows restless, like a flock of water-fowl waiting for a night flight, or a rabbit that smells stoat in the grass. Will they feed tonight, or travel on upriver, or simply play in the shadows, in foreplay of love?

In the dining-room, that same man feels excited as a child again, forced to wait by a fastidious chef, or by his partner who eats too slowly, or even by soup that will not cool. And all this frustration while the colours of the daytime fade away to monochrome and the hum of the twilight insects builds up in the trees. The lights are on behind their shades and crystals, and there looks back at him his face, reflected from the window pane. The late night, non-fishing diners are on their way . . . it must be time to leave.

Everything is packed, made up, laid out, ready for the journey into the estate, now darkening above the Lyd. Rabbits are playing on the track, the fields to the river are already sheened with mist. A good night, good luck magpie flies over, lost in twenty yards but for his white wing tips. The purple feather clouds that had gathered around the sun from time to time had

Chris Turnbull 84.

cleared away, blown by a wind that had itself disappeared into
the night sky and then whispered its way out through the stars.

The pool lies under the gloom and disorder of Gathered
Wood. There is a silence there, enough to hear the small brown
trout moving on the shallows, so silent you fancy you hear the
moon above slowly spin in the sky, the owl float in the air or
the mists actually rise from the meadow dips. There is a magic in
the very earth this night.

The reconnaissance of the morning will be repaid. The pool is
a rough figure of eight, an approximate hour glass and there are
three fishing stations on it: a fast run into the pool where a fish
will take like dynamite; a slower top pool, deep on one side and
overhung with trees, shallower on the other where the fish will
come onto the slope of the sandbank. And thirdly there is the
bottom bulge of the pool, deep at the head, widening and
shallowing into the spread of the beech tree, where the otters

Chris Turnbull 84

live, caverned into the roots. But there is no whistle from them tonight. They are travelling the valleys and it is fish that send out the slow spreading ripples across the water.

Plans are run through, bearings are fixed, again the tackle is checked in the light that still dawdles from the day and which is added to now by the rising moon. The fish will soon settle in to a pattern, will feel secure for the night and, by waiting, the angler will only encourage them.

The deep water is hazed with mist, but through it a shape seems to be looming. Surely there are the flashes of turning fishes down there, glinting in the dark. A little after nine, the first lady shears into the sky, long and lean, like a fighter on a night flight. In the silence she is heard, as well as seen, her rush ripping the still air, the tearing of water droplets along her body, the sprays from her fins forming a momentary vapour trail behind her. Her life seems to belong as much to the sky as to the water; she is transformed into a sleek silver bird that reaches a zenith and holds there a second, but turns, falls faster and faster into the water, becoming grey once again, and loses that heavenly splendour. A fish now, she marks her return to the depths by a string of glowing bubbles, until they too burst and nothing more remains.

Slow, short casts at first, that let the big flies down only five yards off, gradually build up to ten or fifteen yards and work arcs around the pool, searching, probing, experimenting with depths and speeds as they go. The casts are working through the sea trout; they register nips, pulls even, from careful fish, too long from the sea, curious, but shy, coming short of the feathers. Cute ladies, willing to play with danger, teasing and laughing as they come out of sleep. Changed flies are equally mocked, as though not a fish will make a mistake, though happy to pretend she might.

At 11.00 p.m. the beech tree becomes the centre of all movement. Fish under the branches are bolder, taking insects loudly and greedily from the surface; the ripples have never let up an instant since dusk, but there is one way only through the branches that the line must follow if it is to land a fly at the heart of the matter. The route was charted in the daylight and trial casts were successful, though, in the dark, distances are deceptive and it is an attempt that is desperate and last ditch.

If the line flies right, it will drift the big Coachman round with the current where the fish are and where it will be hit like a blast of dynamite, by a fish of fury.

It is. The rod slashes over and the line slaps away through the rings, attached to one of these superb creatures from the sea, of the night, in contact with the wild. The trout is going to fight with its head, and its heart. The two piece is the nearest yet to its death, a black rapier hoop, and the fly line daggers down.

This is fishing now, in the moonshine water, lightning flashed by the fish on her broad side, rubbing her head on the rocks, a Houdini of escape.

The rod has just enough to get her away from the bottom. So, she fights in the sky. As she hurdles, the rod bounces. Seven times. A tight dance and neither can escape it.

She tries to make bottom and cannot. She tries to leap and falls back. She seeks to stay stable, and leans to her side. She is all up. Bent in the net, she is unhooked, staring at her fate.

When I placed her back in the shallows I feared, really feared, that she was too far gone, that her heart had burst in her silver belly. Twice she rolled onto her back. Both times I lifted her upright even if her gills worked hardly at all. Then the breath came in gulps and spasms. That limp body then tremored and juddered, and up and down it the nerves worked, re-tightened, recharged, as though the thrill to be free was still alive in her brain.

Another half an hour, I lay with her, as her head began to work, as her pectorals bent firmly in co-ordination, till her tail thrashed and with a surge of power she threw off my fingers and plunged away from man forever.

The pool had gone very quiet now. It was past midnight. Daylight was only four hours off so I sank into the bank, pulled my coat around me and slept. A fitful sleep, for though I was tired, the river was with me and as night disappeared, cold and mist settled once more.

So it was that dawn came dream-like: night and day, sleep and waking, were dovetailed into one another. Perhaps in truth I was quite asleep. Perhaps none of my visions were real, but I still feel I saw the forest, pewter grey, swept by mists. Deer, like wraiths, flitted on the limit of my sight, just beneath the beech tree, all but silent, fairy beings that trotted on a sigh of the wind or that could skip on the water itself. Perhaps I rose from the stones, or coughed, but the images blurred, the animals melted into the forest and I sank back into sleep.

The Wolf

He was out long before dawn, because the midsummer night was never remotely dark for him, because the bright days he might as well fill with sleep as with fishing. Days were useless for him; dusk and parts of the night till dawn he really could do something. The mist formed about sun up, or a little before, so deep and so grey that he was made invisible, his greyness absorbed into the greater greyness. Erect, controlled, the Master Fisherman waited and watched out for a fish he knew would come. He caught two in fact, but as the sun rose higher it drew the mists towards it. The water cleared to vanishing point and a trout now could see a pinhead in infinite space. Ambush and surprise had been made a total impossibility. For the fourteen hours of sunshine, all fish would become untouchable. The Master knew it and accepted it. Had there been a drizzle, or broken cloud, or a breeze to put a ripple on the water then he would have fished on, and, with his skill, would have been successful. But this was another Sahara day, to be slept through. So he left the water, and closed one eye tight. But the other he kept a mite open, just in case of change. Just in case. A Master never lets go.

He was well away. The air became thick and warm like milk. Where the Wolf meets the Thrushel the hills crowd around; they cradled the heat – heat that was real, something you could touch. The cattle sheltered in the shade of hedgerows. The sloping hay meadow was harvested and sleepy rabbits lollopped off, to a change of address, hardly half bothered. Nothing moved unless it had to, and even necessity was half paced.

Between them, the Wolf and the Thrushel were hard put to it, to form a river. Their junction pool barely moved: a sliver of water slipped away downstream, evading the rocks, nowhere near capable of covering them. All the fish had gathered there of course, for at least some shade, some depth, some oxygen, but they were a bad tempered lot. The big fish lay deep and sulked, and only the little fish moved at all, snapping at this and that under the trees on the Thrushel bank. The Master Fisherman was well, well away.

One big trout did however move that day, leaving the shade where the water was dead slow and drifting into the tail of the pool where the water was faster with a hint of ripple to it, with a lack of oxygen, with a memory of life there. He was a fine fish – ten pebbles long and weighed over a pound. A native, river born and bred, and no doubt he was a few summers wise.

His body was too deep for such thin water: the action of his fins and body on the silt and algae-covered stones had cleaned them bare. His favoured lying places dappled a ten yard area like bone china saucers. The top tip of his tail waved clear of the surface, and his adipose and all his dorsal, which he unfurled lazily above him from time to time, like a lady uses a fan in the heat.

It was impossible for a man lying there on the stones to move for his rod. He tried, but the first mumble on the stones and the fish showed obvious alarm. The angler's muscles relaxed him back to where he lay, for to watch is as pleasant as to fish, and, the beauty of holidays, the day was his own to do with as he wished. So the made up rod, leaned against the ladder to the pool five yards away, went unused.

At times the ten pebble trout lay no more than three or four feet from the angler's nose – like the cartoon of a cat watching a canary – and every action of the fish could be seen: its steady eye movements; the working of the fins to maintain position, the body corrections too; the water fleas that disappeared into the fish's mouth and were absorbed without shadow of jaw movement. Bigger nymphs were ignored. It was not a day for feeding, but for attempting to win what comfort a trout could out of it all on that river bed of dried out stones. Darkness would do for hunting.

It was a magnificent sunset: blues, crimsons, oranges and yellows all in a cauldron of fire. The margins of the river began to fill in with shadows and blacken out. The Master Fisherman returned: his entry to the tail of the pool was quite perfect. He kept the light of the falling sun to his side so that no shadow was cast onto the water, even though he could still see through the surface film to what might move beneath. His arrival was quiet enough not to disturb a stone, dislodge a seed from the clumps of willow herb or even send a ripple over the pool to announce his presence. He was like death in the night.

He could afford to wait. No sign of impatience ruffled him for he was at one again with the river, and time and the setting sun were on his side now. The trout in the pool were once more vulnerable, now they would move more, betray themselves as the rise began.

The ten pebble trout that had been alarmed by the departing angler and had fled, could not have known about the arrival of the Master to the pool. So, as the air cooled and mist formed on the slower pools and over the uncut meadows, the fish returned to his shallows.

Now he was feeding, digging for nymphs, but in only a few inches of water, still quite aware of flies over the top of him. As time passed, so the fish became more and more engrossed, less and less vigilant, more and more the glutton. The Master observed all this and grew certain of his prize.

What saved the trout was the moon, up early, hanging a silver

orb in his upper eye. And when that eye saw the image of the moon sliced, saw the rapier thrust of blackness blur across the ivory face, the message to the brain and then to the powerful caudal fin was instantaneous. The trout thrashed away in a flurry of foam and spray that leapt up to meet the dagger beak that now stabbed past into the empty shingle of the river bed.

The Master's crawks of rage filled the valley and on slow lumbering wings he took off to the heronry on the estuary where life would be easier perhaps and where he could get away from what seemed to him to be the derisive hoots of the owls. Unharmed he was, but the ten pebble trout had marked the dangers of the shallows well. When I found him again the next day, he was twenty yards upstream in deeper water and showed not the slightest inclination to go back there again.

The Carey

For some reason, I could not sleep the night before my visit to the
Carey. The moon was near full so perhaps it was the silver light
that flooded the room which disturbed me. And neither was
there the slightest shift of breeze, so just as annoying was the
close air and the clammy bedclothing. As I lay there, mind
river–drifting, I became aware of sounds in the roof above my
head. They were soft for the most part, as though the tiles were
being lifted slightly, examined and being replaced gently again,
as though an owl had lost the key to his door, and were searching
high and low, anxious to get home before dawn. There were
frequent, long pauses and then the shuffling and tapping would
begin again. Here and there it seemed as if the plaster, or straw,
or both were being dislodged and falling onto the ceiling itself.

I feared rats or mice but soon realised the sounds were too
measured, too controlled to be any feverish rodent. I thought
back to when a bat had begun to hang inside my bedroom
window frame, but its scuffles in no way resembled the sinister
progress of this creature now.

The last disturbances came from directly overhead. The same
shuffling and knocking of clay on clay that seemed so loud in the
otherwise still night. But now, all of an instant, in the dead
hours, havoc broke loose. A war was being fought above me.
There was such a beating and thrashing in the roof space that the
plaster rained down. Screeching. Screaming. Total silence. Tip-
toes on the tiles towards the window.

Looking in for a second, the moonlight bright around her, was
the cat on the sill, in her mouth a starling. I rose and watched her

as she rippled over the lawns into the dappled silver shade of the orchard. The hunted must never sleep. This I remembered the next day on the Carey. With a vengeance.

When I did sleep, it was deeply, engulfing the alarm clock: the dawn patrol had turned into a mid-morning stumble. There was a drought on the country, yes, but Devon still looked fresh enough that morning with hills as green and pleasant as any you could imagine, enclosed by neat walls, dotted with gleaming white, prosperous farmhouses, and wandered overall by chubby, trim sheep.

A drought, though, was evident enough in the state of the river. The Carey looked nothing more than a tear drop running on the bone hard earth. The stickles had shrunk until the pebbles had their backs bleached. If the pool ever had depth or green tinged colour, then both had vanished long before. Here evidenced the fury of the summer, trickled the proof that rain had not fallen since April. The river was reduced to a liquid nothing. An excuse, with trout in it.

They were trout, more successful than that starling, which never slept, that saw me thirty yards downstream of them and probably sensed me earlier than that. They were trout that would not be fooled by a fly even attached to the hair of an angel, trout that could feel the swish of the rod disturb the still air, even before they saw the shadow of it above them. They were living eight inch bars of wariness and distrust, networks of quivering senses, fish that trembled at their shadow, whose eyes roamed from quadrant to quadrant day and night and never blinked, let alone closed. They were trout that fled before a swallow, which could be disturbed by the kick of their own tail.

I fished for them as well as I could. I did all the right things. I kept low. I kept on the move, and then with considerable caution. I fished with gear as light as human manufacture allows, and cast as far off as I could whilst still keeping perfect control. In fact, I fished as well as I have ever done, but for trout that had long since left the water space before me. I could as well have fished in a bath.

On a pool neck that I crept to, I scared four trout that spun off

to all points of the compass, in heron confusing zigzags. Deciding on an ambush, I dug in there, into the bankside, to await their return, line out, fly on, quite ready. They did not, however, return, not in an hour at least.

When I did see a trout over a run of gravel and it stayed there, I feared it was dead, but I put on a Pheasant Tail, tied tiny and cast to it. Everything went out perfectly, and the nymph rode the current down to the fish. He saw it, closed, and the decision was made in a blur of movement so quick I could not think of reaction. As my wrist jerked instinctively, the fly was again riding on its way, down a barren river, and all I did was to tangle in the brambles. I never even saw the trout leave.

Putting a fish on the bank now seemed even further away from me. In every river elsewhere, the drought of the summer had made trout languid but here the lack of water had resulted in hyperactivity, in fish electrified by a sound or shadow, tense as their streams dried around them. It was as though the word had gone down the river that things were serious, and that they all knew it.

For me, I was desperate for a while. On her way to execution, the hair of Marie Antoinette turned snowy white, but here what I felt was the desperation of strength-sapping inertia, alternating with the rage of impotence and frustration. Eventually, I was simply lethargic, knowing the hopelessness of anger, and the uselessness of optimism. I was riddled with the knowledge of absolute failure, a mental failure, a skill failure and a physical failure. A Carey eight incher seemed as far away as the stars. Even if I were to wait until the darkness came, the night was full mooned and they would see me just as well in silver as in gold.

And then I relaxed – notice this latest stage in the beaten angler's psychological development – I relaxed because I knew I was in the great world, where nature decreed, not I, what would or would not be. I could not make the stars shine, or the earth turn, or summon up the clouds from the sea. I could only act on what I found, and I had done my best. Happier after this personal mind game, I took off upstream.

There was a wood and, a hundred yards into it, a pool where

the fish seemed to forget the drought and were feeding steadily and with obvious satisfaction, like all trout should. The pool was roughly half moon shaped, deep on my side where the bank was thickly wooded and quite impenetrable. An immature oak tree stood at its head where the thin water entered and a fallen holly bush spread at its tail, happy there until the winter flood moved it on. Only from the far bank could I hope to put in a cast, and through the tanglewood, I cut a way, looking for a crossing place.

I experienced the full fury of the wild wood to protect its own. Furious at disturbance, it flung nettles at my chest, brambles at my arms, and thistle down my boots; it summoned up a wasp into my shirt and mosquitoes onto my brow. But I overcame the forest, and heart beating, sick and giddy I got there, lurching into the willow herb that crowded the pool's bank.

There were twenty fish before me, nothing large, but, you will guess, that did not matter then. The wild wood still watched. I checked on the arc of the back cast, computing on how it would thread through the raging branches of the holly and bramble. I looked again to focus on the area of busiest activity and I realized that the trout were happy everywhere. I had only to get a fly those seventy or so inches into the water.

The Coachman, tied on a size 20, dimpled into the neck of the pool, hugged the surface film a second and sank in a stream of smaller than pin-head bubbles. The most confident trout I have ever seen made a big mouth at it and turned away chewing, with the cast following. It looked six inches, but then airborn, twice, three times, more like an eight incher. And once beached, I awarded myself the honour of a takeable Carey fish, and returned it. I still had the wild wood trail to retrace!

Back in the real world, in the here and now of open meadow, the river was as it had been, full of never sleeping trout jittery at the sound of their heart beat. I brooded on the magic of the pool in the wood. Perhaps so far into the wood, it kept a lower temperature, perhaps with lower light values. Perhaps there the fly life was different and more active on bright days. Many trout had gathered there and perhaps the confidence of one had spread to others and then the urge to feed had passed through them all. The pool was probably unfished and perhaps the fish were simply naive and unsuspecting.

The virgin pool of innocence, that was one of my lucky breaks that whole summer.

The Barle

Trout fishing can transcend time, and people and continents. It can be developed to become a form of art, a branch of philosophy and a way to love. A man who takes up trout fishing as a pastime only, understands a mere half of it all, if that even, but at least he is on the way and need only open up his mind a little to appreciate the beauty of what he does, to become quite apart from the common man. To a few, fishing for trout has become a way of life itself, one that has fulfilled them to the core. It has solved secrets for them, introduced them to essential truths and has led them to their dreams.

The answer to all this is that fishing for trout, the whole experience of it, can be beautiful, and the deeper a man wades, the more beautiful it seems to him. Until, at the last, he will go to the ends of the earth for that ultimate beauty. Lest you think that all this is fanciful, let me tell you about somebody I once knew, whom I last met on the river Barle, and then you can decide.

When I was a young child, a traveller came periodically to our home. His appearances signalled the start of exotic times, embroidered with colourful presents, and strange smelling perfumes and tobaccos. The traveller was tanned, always wore white as I remember, and talked with my parents hours into the night whilst I lay above them, believed to be asleep. Sometimes he showed photographs, prints of smoking volcanoes, of villages devastated by earthquake, fire or flood, of temples, of castles, seas, mountains and rivers as wide as the world itself.

To me, then, he was a fabulous being, who landed on us when his star came in and who left as if to other planets. At the end, we

expected him, then half expected him and finally half forgot him, and for fifteen years I knew no more about the traveller.

In 1972, however, searching through family papers I came across a last letter from him, dated ten years before, with an address and enclosing a drawing of a West Country cottage, standing beside water. I wrote, received a reply and left the next springtime to see the traveller once more.

We fished all day on the Barle, his local river, which ran almost by his door. He was a wizard on it, in that fast broken water for the tiny, rocket-quick trout. Though he seemed frail to me, we walked and fished for miles, until in the late afternoon we came to a pool beneath the Tarr Steps, where the Bronze Age engineers had flung their mule bridge across a shallows and where it has stood against flood into forever.

In and around that pool he gave me an exhibition of river fishing I will never forget. Over twenty yards he picked up a trout in front of, or behind, every rock that he came to. Each time his fly crossed the current a fish wheeled at it, and he never missed a take.

Whilst I struggled to land three fish, my companion had a dozen, and those over a shorter length of water than I was

Chris Turnbull 84.

fishing. This I put down to his casting which was quite pin–point; to his movements which were as gentle as the swaying oaks on the cliff face opposite; to his knowledge of the river for I noticed that he stood only on the rocks that would carry his weight and avoided those that would have tipped me into midstream; to his choice of fly, or at least his working of them, for no trout ever looked like refusing. Without these rational answers, the power my friend had over the river would have seemed unnatural, but even with them, I realised I fell short of full understanding.

He would not stop fishing until dusk. He could not, he said, let a minute go unused at his age, which I believe was well over seventy. At last we walked through the heavily wooded valley, where the owls screeched, the long way home.

After dinner he told me that I had been fortunate to catch him before his next journey, his return to the trout streams of Kashmir, where he had not fished since the 1920s. This time, as he had then, he was attempting the overland route there, by road and rail. To me, then as now, this seemed an evil prospect of discomfort and frustrating slowness, but to him it offered a study of peoples across continents, all a part of his fishing.

His plans were to reach the State in the autumn, when the snow waters had run off and the rivers were left as low and transparent as Alpine streams. He described the rivers there as flowing from springs out of the rock face, or from the high lakes and glaciers or even those solely snow fed. Access to many of the trout reaches had taken days in the twenties, had involved him in small scale treks with Western civilisation left very far behind.

There was one special river he yearned to re-visit, a stream that ran in the foot-hills of great mountains and which could only be reached on foot, so remote was the area. He had passed many days there half a century before and he had never forgotten one detail of it since.

He described it so wonderfully as to remind me of that Heaven Socrates saw just before his death. The traveller had been fishing a river of ice water that was clearer than clarity itself, clearer than the tear of a young girl. The skies were blue, but bluer than any other blue and the clouds were white as first day snowdrops. The valley enthralled him as if before he had been blind and could only then see, as though his life had been lived in a mist, as if he himself had been the trout, used to subdued colours and had only now witnessed the real, beautiful world. Here the air was purer and the bird-song sweeter than in his summer dreams. It was an image that had possessed him all his life after leaving it, and even now, just the descriptions of it that he gave me, haunt what I write.

I wondered at the old man as he talked, the full thrill of fishing still in him, the surging force to take him back those thousands of miles to what was for him something more than a wonderful land. As I drifted into sleep in the room kept warm by the chimney breast, and listened to the old man moving beyond the wall, I prayed for him that the trout would still have spots as large and as crimson as cherries, that they would still leap to the mountain tops when they felt his steel, and that the land was still on the way to the foothills of the Gods.

We slept. Or I did, for when I awoke he had left and only a letter remained and a pot of coffee still warm. Gone. The traveller was as magical as ever, his star had called for him once more. I burnt the note in the embers of the last night's fire: it said that he hoped to return within three years, but I heard no more.

[103]

In 1984, on a glorious summer evening, I again fished the Barle and as dusk settled into the valley I went again to his cottage. There were new people there, no, not new, different, for they had been there ten years and had cleared away all the travellers belongings. Only one book of his remained, which they were good enough to give me. It was a volume he had showed me my one night there, the *Angler in Northern India*, published in 1917, and annotated by the traveller himself with footnotes he had made whilst in Kashmir, much as I make my notebooks now.

The next day, I slipped the book in my tackle bag and wandered with it to the Tarr Steps and down to the pool of his introduction. In his very memory I fished the place as hard as I could. The two piece was built for this work and purred at it all, would have said 'thank you' if it could. Still, it let its eight feet do the talking and this day I had seven trout where I had once taken the three, where he had once had the dozen, and I felt better with myself, with time enough to watch the buzzards mewing over the ridge, riding on the flows of warm air.

At the neck of the pool a cluster of rocks makes something like an armchair and I settled into it happily and reached for the book. The spine was badly cracked, but the good strong linen binding had seen it hold over countless miles and God knows what roughness of terrain. The tiny pencil written notes were made alongside a dozen, wild sounding streams, on the Achabal, the Wangot, the Arrah and more. They recorded fish hooked, lost and landed and one weighed at over six pounds with a 'head on it like a leopard'.

There were descriptions of the Doonge House Boat, of the watermen of sixty odd years ago, of Fakroo, Fakira, Sher, Hasan and all, trout men of another continent, all dead now unless India is more wonderful than we know. Men of the generation of the old rod now rested with me on the sand, all belonging to a life long gone, quick as a blink of the eye.

The traveller was never rich, for he would rather risk all for

fish and adventure. He was willing to be poor for years, and he was so. He left nothing but my book. Everything was within him and to know him was something. I wondered if he caught on that last journey, if the dear old man with hair white as the Himalayan snows was successful. Or wilder, I dream some nights that he is still there in his heaven, transformed, preserved eternally in his bliss. I awake half expecting him to call and I fancy that if his star should reappear, what a trout fisherman's story we should all have.

The traveller with the two piece . . . I am a pale image of that man.

DERBYSHIRE AND THE NORTH

An Introduction

I moved on to Derbyshire and the northern rivers by way of the Welsh Borderlands. My purpose was to fish with a long-time friend on the River Severn for barbel, both as a break from trout and the fly and to relive some happy times there. Everything went well. On the crack of a mist filled dawn I settled into a favourite barbel haunt I had known well over the years.

My tackle was borrowed. My bait was given, a gallon of hempseed, the black skins still glossy from the pot, cooked until the white shoots began to burst through. To draw the barbel to me, I rained twenty large handfuls into the head of my swim, to drift down through the slow current and lay a carpet on the river's bed.

And then I waited and watched, happy occupations this summer. The river awakened, the sun came up from somewhere behind the Midlands and its rays painted the slow waters grey-green and greasy, pushing a sluggish way southwards. The mystery of the ten foot hole beneath me seemed infinite. Excitement welled up inside me, and the sure knowledge that nothing else in life matters as much as fishing, as much as those barbel sniffing the hempseed down in the depths, nosing their way through the oily water to my very feet.

The river brutes were on their way, I knew it, and then I saw it. In amongst the hazy dawn light, a rosary of bubbles beaded onto the surface as somewhere, deep beneath, the snout of a barbel had tracked down the hemp and was rooting and burrowing there.

More strings appeared, large bubbles, pin-prick bubbles and bubbles that fizzed to a foam. These strange, small eyed, long

whiskered fish had found me, had moved in and were having a party in the swim. My hempseed had created a feeding spree where I could not see, where I could only guess and imagine.

For a hookbait, I used a maggot, eleven feet beneath a red tipped float that inched its way through the hole. On its first run, the float that had been there, simply was no longer. It did not dip. It did not hesitate, but vanished from all view of the world and I found the rod hooped over from tip to butt.

No fight from any trout, sea, brown or rainbow could possibly have been more breath-taking. No fish could have run longer, or deeper or faster than that ferocious barbel from the depths of the murky river, and when at last he came up, no fish could have been more fine, at my feet, in the sunshine. His body was lean, lithe and strong, twisting like a python: his fins were a colour no man but a barbel fisher could have seen before, somewhere between pearl and mandarin: his scales were chain-mail that glowed from a dusky bronze around the shoulders to a salmon pink over the belly. Upright again, breathing well, he became a shadow and with farewell bubbles, departed back to the ten foot hole.

At midday, I left for the next stage of my journey. I returned to the MG and checked over my fly tackle: the two piece and its reinforcement, a stronger rod for any unkind tasks and a small canvas bag of reels, casts, fly boxes, oils and greases. I opened the four boxes to the sunlight and was suddenly overwhelmed with satisfaction that with these strange creatures of steel, fur and feather, I was able to catch most species of fish swimming the English rivers. On a fly, I had taken dace on the Nadder, pike on the Glaven, roach on the Bure and had heard tell of a barbel falling to a nymph on the Avon. To come, chub would take my fly on the Eden, perch on the Till as of course, trout and grayling did everywhere.

The simple two piece and canvas bag had never looked more attractive to me. Compared with the stack of barbel gear, the basket, the bait buckets, rod rests, keepnets and landing nets, they were my freedom of movement, my ability to travel the rivers as I wanted, to take fish as far away as I chose. Indeed, when I reached Derbyshire, I began by walking eight miles of the Derwent, pondering over every pool on my way, eager to reach the next wood or the next rapids I could hear singing in the distance. The old toothpick rod and schoolbag of tackle were no drawback to anything I did, or to the things I wanted to do.

My hands still smelt of the hemp and were discoloured a dark blue. What I had done there, on the Severn, was to create an artificial 'rise'. I had triggered off a feeding frenzy with my tiny seeds that had nothing to do with natural causes. I could not condemn what I had done, the thrill of the battle and my admiration for the defeated fish were far too powerful for that. And yet, I felt a definite confirmation for what was my main purpose of the summer, to catch river trout, and grayling, on a fly.

It seemed more than ever that my sport was a sophisticated dovetailing with nature and its workings. If, on the Severn, I had overwhelmed natural forces and twisted them to my own ends, in my trouting I was attempting to learn to read the forces of a river. Success came when I had flashes of insight into them, and more often I failed, because they were ahead of me, outside my understanding.

[111]

What I was quite sure about was that the whole idea was well worth doing, and in this happy state of mind, I rolled the hood down on the car, and made off for Derbyshire.

Keeper on the Wye

We talked for a while under the porch looking out across the lawns to the river. He examined the two piece for a time long enough to indicate real interest and said it was well whipped and then we walked the river where he showed me good lies for the next day. Good they were, interesting to attempt, full of fish, and I realised a lot lay ahead of me. I thanked him and we drew back to the cottage, from which he led me to the last pool, very large, very deep, full of undercuts, where the limestone had receded inch by inch, century by century, flood by flood.

'In here,' he said, 'are the biggest fish in the Wye.' I believed him.

We sat on the grass bank at the foot of the pool. Opposite us, with gardens tripping to the riverside, were other cottages and behind those rose up one of the moors of the Dale. He told me a thunderstorm was coming, though I could not detect it; but he smelt it in the wind, could tell it from the cloud, he just knew somehow that we would get rain. And this would be just what I wanted, in fact, to freshen up the river for my day's fishing. Such a man was the River Keeper.

At our feet the pool shallowed from a dozen feet, to six, to one and a half, over a couple of rod lengths, and at the start of the shallows hung a twelve ounce brown trout. The Keeper saw it before me, he had this knack, and we watched it for a while. It opened its performance for us by showing what I had not seen before this summer, the somersault take. Can I describe it? The fish was, of course, lying facing upstream and saw float into its range a moth of some sort. The trout's fins and body went quite

all of a quiver. It obviously fancied what it saw. From here its movements were rapid. It swam smartly upstream of the moth and jumped out of the water behind it, turning over the moth in flight. Now, as it re-entered, it both battered the insect with its tail and then dragged it sub-surface. Turning once more in the water, the trout ate the small moth with ease.

For a while after, the trout, although only an average fish, deserved our attention. He took up his position again and began surface feeding quite busily on small olives, I think, coming past him. Each one he inspected over a travel of about four inches before taking. After some minutes, a larger fly came into his window and was at once seen, just as the moth had been earlier. On this occasion, the trout followed it nine inches, let it go another six, and made up the lost water to follow it again another foot and then, eventually, let it go downriver for good. Several times, the fish was on the point of taking the fly. You just felt how much he wanted it. Each time, though, he kept himself in check. The fish, not a cunning old fish of the river, did not trust a fly out of its accepted feeding pattern. Anything within its fly range was, even so, inspected minutely. In just these few minutes, my sky high confidence for the next day was dented.

The Keeper had seen all these trout tricks before. On the Wye, I doubt if any trout anymore could surprise him, for he is near part of the river himself. His work is not work. It is not forty, not a hundred hours long a week. He does not carry a watch, he does not need one. That day, the coming night, the next day, the following years he would always be on the river. Where else would he be? Where else would he be happy, but on the river ever flowing, ever staying? And if he is sad to see a favourite trout taken away, another fills its place. Such is the magic of the river. Such is the watercraft of this man, who can smell a trout I cannot even see.

He is right to be proud of the Wye. It is a remarkable river. Remarkable if only for its natural born rainbows. Their condition is excellent and their colouring fantastic. Best of all is their inquisitiveness. They are all over the river, in the pools, in the shallows, in the eddies, the back eddies, and even foraging in the puddles. Whilst the browns look moody from lack of oxygen the rainbows still make this an active river.

He is proud also of the Wye's water shrimps, which he says breed all year round – there are certainly many of them. He has seen a dabchick choke on a bullhead. He has seen a life come and go in that pretty valley. He told me how one of his fishermen still came to the river in his last summer, when he was painfully ill, hardly able to bear it at times. The Keeper would find him crying with pain, though still fishing, half happy even in agony. Sometimes the lure of an upstream lie would drag him too far from his car and the Keeper would carry him back through the dusk.

He died on a night after he had been to the river. His last evening there had been warm and still, and from the woodland close an owl called over and over, not the clear shriek that knives through a cold night, but a soft bubbling hoot that fills the air with comfort and security, with a feeling that to die on such a night would be a hardship, yes, but yet only a kneeling before time and history wherein all summer nights are filled with silver owls and moons and the late rises of untouched trout.

That man will always have a rod there, in the Keeper's memory. For he was the one man who truly knew how to fish the river. He would fish on the stickles during the day, using to the full the diffused light and the swifter current that give old eagle eyes less time for searching examination. Even in his last days he would get over the gravel and stones in total quiet, put out just a short line and take wholly unsuspecting fish from only a rod length away.

As the light paled and the sun hid behind the moors, only then he would move to the deep pools for the monsters. Fish of three and four pounds came from their underwater ledges and caverns, bitten into the soft limestone. In the quiet water, he had the knack of fishing a pheasant tail neither on the top, nor in the water, but quite literally in the surface film itself. He hardly moved it, only just enough to crinkle the oily sky above the fishes' heads.

The Keeper took the old two piece and showed me exactly what he meant. It was all very delicate fishing and within two casts he registered a solidly positive take that he never even

bothered to tighten up on. It was as if you or I were feeding a pet goldfish for the benefit of a child.

That day he had been watching trout in the deep mid section of the river, some miles below us on the pool here. I had passed the water by. To me it had appeared uninteresting. Little flow and wide, and almost lagoon-like in its placidity, it had smacked not a jot of trout fishing, river trout fishing anyway, which is all lightness and life. Yet, there, the Keeper had watched three very big, still totally natural rainbows, feed. They had worked in unison, a tight team, throwing up a silt cloud. They had gyrated their massive, thick shouldered, small headed bodies into the mud, thrashed into it like eels, beaten their tails onto it and bellied into it until an immense cloud began to form, lift and shift. The three big fish then dropped three yards downstream and began to work hard, feeding off the shower of pickings their activity had caused to appear. Fish, you know, are just as worthy of study as any living creature. They do have rational, functioning minds and as my Keeper so well proved, a man does not need to catch to enjoy them.

There really was thunder in the air and even I could sense it now. Cloud had welled up between the moors. The light in the dale was much subdued and you could smell the rain in the gusty breeze. So, we stirred and wandered to the neck of the pool where it ran shallow, full of strings of weed and small loose stones. Here was one of the favoured spawning sites each year, to which fish made their way from over great distances. Some are big fish, others only just mature and for anything up to a week they writhe in the swift water before dropping back exhausted into the deep pool to rest. In there, some fish died. The herons always knew it and flooded into the dale beforehand, guided by an inbuilt ability to sense destruction and a capacity to communicate to each other, scavenger to scavenger, a disaster or a death on the grand scale.

Wrenching ourselves away another time, we walked on, but still the Keeper could not help looking around his valley. He scanned the hillside above us. He put his binoculars up. There were walkers on the fells. And to him, rightly, this was potentially a disaster. The drought had dried the heather wasted acres up there into a tinder. Not necessarily a dropped match or cigarette, but a metal toe cap clashed against a rock, could result in a fire. And a fire up there, unattended, unattainable, unstoppable meant havoc, would result in horrible destruction.

Then he closed me down, he pulled me to him. There were badgers up there. And in the drought they were having a hard time of it, a very hard time indeed, such as you, or I, do not realise. The dry had sent the beetles, the worms, the food they depended on down deep. And no dews, no puddles, now no mountain trickles and so too, the moisture of the moor had melted away from them. So up there, each night, the Keeper went, with milk, with bread, with scraps of meat, and the badgers came to him, relied on him, their Red Cross saviour in this bleak sun scorched summertime.

At last I felt I had something of my own to tell the man, to tell him how I myself had once befriended a badger of my own.

★   ★   ★

I cannot say exactly where he lived, just in case he ever should return. I would not want to lose his friendship, for he would know who to blame if he found his old home disturbed. He was shy, you see, and I think I was the only one to visit him.

It is a while since we met. From early on a November afternoon I had been roach fishing down on the bottom meadows where the Wensum turns into the copse. You see, I am

[119]

the type of man who will fish for any species in their season. As dusk approached, a rising west wind blew dark clouds over the last low streak of sunset. Spots of rain began to peck the back of my hands; I had a three mile walk back to the cottage. The roach would have a reprieve that night.

I made to move, but it was an effort. I had been still so long among the wet rushes, and as I looked round for the alder branch to help me up I saw a small, low shape coming towards me. I thought it was a dog, perhaps the farmer's old spaniel far from home, and called out to it. The little face looked up, a flash of white cut through the darkness. As graceful as the river, the squat animal wheeled away and darted back into the wood – and after twenty years of life in the country I had seen a badger!

The next afternoon I went to the river early and I searched that wood hard. It still took me an hour before I found the sett under a splayed, fallen oak. A well-worn track led from that deep hollow along the drainage ditch and disappeared towards the meadows and marshes to the South. Another wound northwards up the valley, past the church.

That wood was so quiet, I could hardly believe it held such a precious life. Not a sound but the murmur of the creeping wind, but the light suddenly grew stronger and I looked up through the branches to the sky to see how high the sun was still. Set against it sat a small short eared owl, quite awake, for his ears twitched twice and I knew that life was everywhere in that wood if I learnt how to look for it.

I took my rod and went back to the river, to the same bend and under the same alder as the previous day. But I could not settle. The Wensum moved gently south, only occasionally rippled by a breath of warm westerly wind, and still the roach meant nothing to me. Well before five o'clock I took my tackle down, and stepping through the dark afternoon I made my way into the wood again.

The sett looked quite black, like jet in the damp earth. Turning my face with the wind, twenty yards east into the wood I saw the alder shattered in the summer storm. Ten feet up in its dead branches would be my perch.

Behind me, a silver pathway ran down the river to the rising moon. It would be a light night. By seven o'clock it was a cold one too, and my coat was shiny with dew. But even then a roach rolled in the water below my tree, exploding the water into silver shrapnel. I waited. By eight o'clock everything had grown quiet, though a barn owl swung like a passing shadow over the dark band of kale. Otherwise the wood, the river, the world, slept.

At nine, or a little after, it happened. I thought I heard a noise first. I cannot be sure now for I was not then. A long, black face emerged from the sett. The white streaks on the muzzle made it look like a ghost rising from the earth.

I felt it knew I was there. It smelled the night. It looked at the moon and I saw its coal eyes twinkle. It shook and stretched and went back to the ground. I waited until eleven o'clock, but it showed no more.

Midday, and I was back again. I caught a small diseased roach and left it by the sett door. A day later I looked again and it had gone. This became a pattern. Every day for some months I left some offering by the sett, sometimes fish, sometimes meat, or even a lump of bread. It had always vanished the next evening when I returned.

I began to wonder if he waited for the gifts. One dusk I looked back from the river and there he was on the ridge, watching me. Until it had grown quite dark he stayed, and only moved as I did.

It was that night snow fell – not thickly, but enough to carpet the whole valley and even cover the wet farmyard. At dawn as I went out it was still crisp, though in the meadow dips the grass was shining through. By the sett, on the spot where I had left some bread, the snow was scattered and the pieces gone. Paw marks led down to the river bank. There too, the snow had been moved and the crusts I had left been taken. The marks turned upstream into the valley, now glowing with snow and the coming day. I followed them for three miles, past the church and a white farm, and over two frozen creeks.

But no footmarks returned, and I felt he must have rested, waiting for the short winter's day in a quiet wood or deep down in a neighbour's sett.

But he never did return. My gifts lay untouched. Spring grass covered his wandering pathways.

★   ★   ★

The storm was well on us now. The moor needed it, the river needed it. I knew I would catch trout the next day and, with the keeper's help, so I did.

The Derwent

There are glimpses of canals, and the reflections of mill chimneys lie upon them like bars. Recollections of a first red-eyed tench in Sammy's Pits, a dark shape sucking in bread flake, before the cancerous Manchester overspill filled him over. Some dead roach float at a lock gate, bloated and glazed eyed, and the water lies foul and polluted. Ripples down another canal in winter when a silver bream lays the Red Quill flat and when a European storm kills half of Manchester's football team. Trophies on the wall, hanging there since that first fishing match was won. Memories of the mill pond cradled in hills and weaver's cottage rows, of a pigeon fancier who won good money on the boy champion and his net of small perch.

Mists over the pool where that first carp slobbered in a crust. Gas lamps guttering on the water where a red float dips to the rudd that is weighed and wondered at. Spring on the reservoir where the first Pennine trout comes up for a dry fly and breaks free. Tears on the wind gone by. Shadows of the Cheshire dusk when a chub pulls under a goose quill and lies beaten on the snow.

A Sunday dawn, shovelled tired eyed onto the charabanc and taken to the Trent. A first gudgeon, a whiskered struggling fish that escapes through the holes of the keepnet. The first baffling experience of current and trotted float tackle that ends in tangle and despair. Threepence, that forgotten octagonal treasure piece, for the driver on the way home. A journey redolent with beer, mouthing songs when you do not know the words, laughing when you do not understand the jokes.

[123]

Chatsworth House

A half way pull-in, at Chatsworth, everyone lying on the rolling hillside above, watching the Derwent at dusk, the trout rising and the mist plume from a fountain. More beer bottles in the grass and cigarette smoke blown out against the midges. Realisation of a different world, of different fishing, of new exciting grandeur. But, forget it boy, back on the coach with you, back into the cities. Another dream half buried with the other fine times and bad, lying half remembered in sleep sometimes, or half recovered on mild midge soaked evenings.

Imagine, twenty-five years on, standing on that same hillside, gazing at that same facaded eternity, watching the same evening rise and seeing the same fountain spray, as if for ever, as if time had never passed, as if the charabanc had never gone away. But now, there is a fishing ticket for the next day in a Barbour breast pocket, and the ghost of memory will be kind and the boy will return triumphant.

Mind games at a child's bedtime in a boy that has no use or desire for sleep. Bars of sunlight still on the bedroom wall and then the first stars appearing through the curtains. There is a fox barking in the wood and an insect flying again and again at the window pane. Too warm for sleep and there are voices in the garden, and someone is playing a piano. Behind tight closed eyes the float dips over and over and small silver fish struggle in the darkness. Deep in the mind, fishing will not let you go.

Twenty-five years on again, tonight an adult decides to go on up to bed. Still it is summer, though now bedtime is your own, not someone else's idea, and you are tired but still sleep will not come. An alarm clock chatters away. Its neon hands move through the night as your mind races away to the dawn, to Chatsworth, to where reality will come at last, after such a long wait.

Where I had always dreamed of fishing through those years, of actually landing a trout, was in the pool beneath the bridge by Queen Mary's Bower. It was that lie on the Chatsworth Derwent that I had fixed my eyes upon first and it was there the dream had to be exorcised.

So, though I walked in front of that magnificent palace as the

[125]

dawn broke, and caught trout from both the lower weir pools, it was to the bridge that I knew I had to return, even if the slower water meant harder fishing. I was making life no more difficult for myself than that dream had always done.

The Derwent was wide, deep and almost still at the bridge. Through films of mist the sun was rising, and blessedly, with it began to blow a breeze. At first it was a riffle and then it was a rush, and brown trout began to appear on the surface, enjoying the new found oxygen, even if not yet feeding noticeably.

I knelt in the sandbank, looking up to the hill. I put on a light tippet and an Olive Nymph tied on an 18 hook, the size no doubt, I had used for those Trent gudgeon that long ago day. My first cast was a good one, settling like a charm right up to the far parapet, and I began to retrieve at much the same speed as the current itself. The fly drifted three inches sub-surface into the area of the moving fish.

Time began to slow down for me, as it always does as tension mounts. The growing wind that had first held up the river now stopped it. Everything was still, time and water. There was no movement in my universe during that one half minute, as though I had always been there, and always would be, frozen like the statues on the bridge or the mansion behind me.

Back in reality, the trout took quickly, though in my numbed state, the movement seemed slow enough, just like an accident you replay slowly over again in your mind. The speed of the trout was on one plane only. I was on another and my strike took him wholly by surprise, and now snapped out of my trance, shocked me at least as much.

He was a lovely fish that I beached, held up against the backdrop of Chatsworth, just a second, till the sun caught it, and then let go. You see he had freed me from that dream and I could only free him in return.

The Wharfe

For a while, for a change, I write straight from my notebook:

'It is Bolton Abbey on a five a.m. sunrise. Fishing the up-stream glide from the stepping stones. In front of the Chancel, bare ribbed, picked clean by time. Like a whale. On the beach of this Wharfe meander. Sunlight on the stone, tripping on the tracery, soothing the frost wounds. Masonry with heart and soul, with tears gone by. The graveyard is full of men been here before.

I cannot catch. My fishing is a ruin. I cannot come to terms here. The river is clear but no clearer than I am used to this summer. But the difference is that it is thinner. Yes, thinner. Less weed, less cover, less body to it; no way can I use the water in my deception of its trout. It exposes me, my leader, my knots, my clumsy casts, it makes me out an alien. Thin, no, this is a mean river to me. If I catch on a fly today it will be despite it, without a shred of help from it. In this most beautiful dale of nothing but meadow, trees, moor and blue sky, the Wharfe has simply cut me down dead.

And nothing upstream, nothing around the island beneath Posforth Gill, or where the stream enters out of the Valley of Desolation, or where the water shoots through the Strid. Nothing. Nothing. Nothing.

I fail on size 14 hooks at five o'clock, 16 hooks at six, 18s at seven, and 20s at eight. My leader has gone from two pound to one. Wouldn't I need to pick a spider's web out of the dew to go lighter . . .'

In that one morning I ran the length of the fisherman's horizon, quietly confident I was, quietly optimistic I became, then inwardly pessimistic and at the last, openly in despair. And yet, if a man keeps trying, keeps at it, something, sometime, might happen for him.

And so it came about that in a mid afternoon I knocked on the door of the father of a friend. He welcomed me in, where it was cool at last out of the sun. The house was a former mill, built of stone, on all levels, to a great height overlooking the same river.

He led me onto a balcony, thirty feet above the water itself, and there beneath, in a long clear pool, lay many trout and grayling. Now strangely, all the fish beneath me were feeding. This was curious, because the trout I had seen elsewhere for five hours past had been round eyed asleep. I admitted I was puzzled.

My new friend took me out of the mill, away from the river, and up the hillside behind, to where a spring gushed out of the rock, in the shade of a tree. It formed a pool like a mirror where flies danced, and then it overspilled down the moorside. For over a hundred feet this ice cold water fell down waterfalls, bubbling through pocket handkerchief pools until it finally splashed cool still and oxygen filled into the tired, milk warm Wharfe beneath the balcony. The force of it had created a pool there, where the water was always as alive as May time, even when the rest of the river sagged around it. That was my lie of magic that day, to find

this oasis in a desert of parched, stale water. Over the following three hours I simply watched trout, mostly through polaroids, but even through binoculars at times, so clear was that ice pool, to make out the finest details.

Six good fish kept together. The dwindled current of the dry summer allowed them to behave much like stillwater fish and they patrolled a well-defined beat rather than maintaining any lie in particular. The fish tracked an orbit of around ten yards, and after each circumference they would rest, perhaps for ten or even fifteen minutes. During these periods they were invisible to the naked eye, they had effected a total vanishment and through the field glasses only could they be picked out, stock-still on the bottom. Only their eyes moved, periodically rolling over, white in their sockets.

Their rest over, they all re-emerged together, quite simultaneously, even though they had been separated from each other in the pool by rocks or gullies and could not keep in visual contact. The shoal instinct is something too deep, too secret to understand, but in these natural bred river fish, probably of a good age, it is well developed and complete, an integrated security system that defies human logic.

As the six patrolled, they fed, always that particular day on the bottom. Through the glasses I could watch them plainly. Shrimps were favourite. A decent crayfish got in its backward, scuttling escape, but three smaller ones did not. They fixed onto snails on the underneath of stones, and drove at them with great power, turning on their sides, working with all their fins and body thrusts for greater momentum as they pushed, scraped and levered with their tight clamped jaws. The image of trout as the languid aristocrats of the stream, sipping in flies, served always by the river, is quite wrong. Here they were working as hard for their food as any diligent bream shoal. Perhaps the only difference was that at least they were being more selective than merely sucking in mouthfuls of silt, sifting for food and bellowing out the dross.

The six were an impressive phalanx. Very boldly coloured, with broad strong heads and bodies that tapered quickly to big,

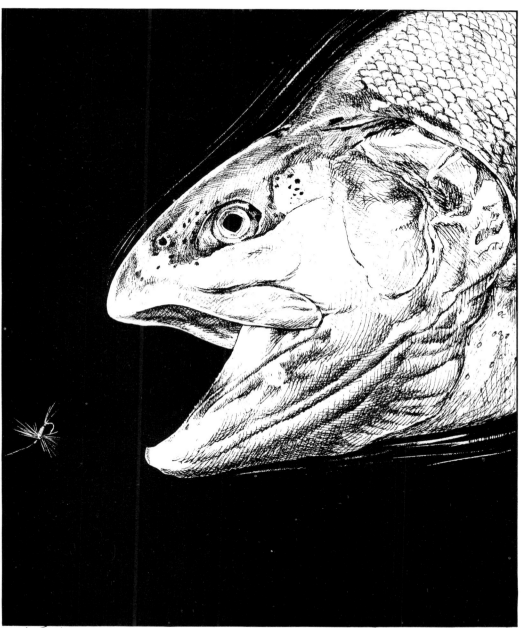

Chris Turnbull 85.

[131]

well-formed caudal fins. Right above them as I stood, their pectorals which seemed exceptionally large, could clamp them firmly to a rock face within a second, or could drive them through the water with one powerful stroke.

My friend told me to fish. These trout were not pets. They were untameable, only here for this staff of life, his spring, not for his table hand-outs. I said I would wait until the light faded, until I could no longer see them. Though taking a visible fish is the highest thrill of angling, in this case I did not find the idea desirable. It was as though knowing their routines as I did, gave me an unfair edge in some way. Of course I was wrong. Even when darkness edged in, hiding my line, masking the workings of the cane rod, I would find them very difficult indeed . . .

Still on the balcony, we watched a goldness come into the sky and shadows fill the gullies of the hillside and trace the rambles of the long stone walls. Over our heads, beneath us and alongside us and around and around us the swallows began to appear, wheeling so close it was as if we too were creatures airborn. We could all but feel the swoop of those tiny frames of bone and feather on our cheeks, weightless almost for a life on the wind, as though they could be carried for ever on those graceful wings. Feathered limbs, so aeronautically perfect, able to fan, to glide and then beat faster than any shutter speed, able to carry those pockets of flesh over mountains, deserts, plains and seas, to Spain, Northern Africa and even finally to the Cape. Birds with a forked tail, which act as both a rudder and a stabiliser; birds that know the magic of the secret of catching insects in flight; birds with superb timing, with eyes well spaced, beaks of great capacity; birds that have bodies capable of great speed and instinctive decision.

We were surrounded by swallows, those graceful hunters, lovely insect eaters, those trout of the airways. Not till the last of them had given way to the night, did I try a cast or two. I forgot that I still had on the fragile leader of the morning and the first pull smashed it within a yard. I could not bother to tie on another. It had been sixteen hours since that Bolton Abbey sunrise.

The Eden

The only hiccup in my time on the Eden was the daylight hours. I caught a chub. I failed to catch any trout at all from a vast quarry pool, from the pool underneath a main line railway bridge, or even from the tail of a sandbank, miles upstream where the valley was so lonely a man could shout and shout and hear only his voice roll back to him from the hills. But, for all the rest, I will never forget a moment: not the night drive across the Pennines, not the rise on the evening of my first day and certainly never my meetings with the master of the river. All these were tinged with something like magic and had that skim of star–dust on them that I believe all river fishermen seek.

I drove in the very early morning when it was still half dawn and half still a gusty night over the Pennines: across the hills from Yorkshire the windscreen wipers had swished, swiped every wind of the way. It had been a tiring journey for the old sports car: the oil light had flickered on and off over the miles, throwing an amber glow over the close, dark cockpit. The gauge had fallen fast as the car heated and hurtled on towards the Eden. It was a summer night in the Northern Counties, but still the fan was on against the cold wetness: 5.00 a.m., but still the headlight beams caught the cat's eyes wriggling home across the moor.

A tired disc jockey played the last of the easy night sounds to the lone, low slung car that growled out at the heather covered hills. Though the night was not done, I braked hard for a lost hare that blinked stupified at the monster that approached. Red and yellow dashboard lights glared as the car lurched, and the tyres bit in hard. The hare made off as the headlamps dimmed, as the car was coaxed back into uncertain life.

As the night waned, big birds hung in the sky, black against the grey, wet from the rain that rolled in from over Ireland way. Sheep were grazing now. A dead one in the road caught the lights in his eyes and the slipstream in his fleece as I went by quick as a bat hurrying against the dawn. Around sunrise mats of blue burst into the sky, and they became patches, and then held hands from horizon to horizon until at 6.00 a.m., I pulled up, rolled back the hood, and rode on down the steaming hillside in full sunlight. Down the same moors I went that in my Beatrix Potter memory Pigling Bland had fled from, with his Pig Wig, until they reached the river, and had crossed it hand in hand. And it was to that river I knew I was going.

★   ★   ★

I do not know when it began, but when I rounded that last corner by the church, close by the farm, I could not quite believe my eyes. As far as they could see, which was for a half a mile, the Eden appeared to rain with trout. There were heavy rises literally everywhere. I had never seen a rise like this one before. I had never guessed such a thing was possible in the realms of nature and reality.

This river that had been so hard, whose shallows had seemed so empty, looked now to be more fish than water, an astounding, amazing morass of trout. Either this was the Eden transformed, or I had walked on to a different river. No matter what, this activity in the shadow of the ancient church was quite incomprehensible to me. It was as though all the olives in the world had been called up to Westmoreland, and been chased by all the trout from all the rivers there.

It was as though the river were not wide enough, or deep enough, or long enough to hold them, but that they had to jump clear, clamber over each other, simply fight for breath. After what I had endured these hours, I was like a child who had seen Santa, the rise was like gold to a forty-niner. It was as though the

valley were turned upside down, the river were running back-
wards, the train on the viaduct were bound for Calcutta not
Carlisle, as though all the reality of the day had gone, as though
brave new worlds had come at last. I had simply never seen a rise
like it.

Winds that blow all day either die at dusk or not at all, and
whine on through the night, through the dark trees and grasses.
The wind that day had calmed and as a result the temperature had
risen. Some clouds had appeared, soft clouds, just enough to add
a velvet touch to the evening. The Eden Valley and the Westmoreland hills no longer seemed such a large place: the moors
closed in, even the sky looked to have dropped a few thousand
miles. The olives were summoned because it was now at last a
warm, intimate place for them.

With my first two casts I had two fish, in seconds of each other,
and their splashing on a tight line was no more desperate than
that of their brothers free around them. The rise, if anything, was
intensifying. I began to move like a man in a nightmare, casting
longer lines, carelessly and hurriedly, scaring fish, once a dozen
fish in one cast that furrowed away up the shallows.

In the shadow of the church itself, I began to steady myself;
think more and move less. I sank my mind into that last twenty
minutes of fishing with a fuller concentration than I had ever felt
before. Though the saturated Orange Quill spread-eagled in the
gloom ten yards off was hard to see, it was as if the intensity of
my feeling projected my mind over the water to it. I heard the
slurp the trout made at it, and though there was no movement on
the line, my body sensed the fly had gone. This total oneness
with my sport lasted some four or five minutes at this peak, and
then deserted me.

I struck, not tightened, at the take. The water boiled like a
cauldron. There was a hammer on the rod, a knife through the
line and the two piece bounced back straight against the evening
sky.

★   ★   ★

Looking down the street to the market place, all the roofs and colours had first been washed by the overnight rain and then polished brightly by the sunshine. A small town of people who know each other, it has the spirit of its hills around, and the music of the river running through it, so that a countryman feels quite at home there. The town is here to serve the countryside, not to dominate or destroy it. There is still an eighteenth century balance between street and fell. It is tucked into the elbow of northern England, held in the hand, Appleby in Westmoreland.

People are buying in for the winter already – their clothes, their boots, provisions – for it will come, despite the warm sun now drying the fine street off for them; it will come with blizzards and gales and days of Atlantic rain when the sheep die and the cart-tracks are impassable for days, when the river rises to the graveyard toes of the old church and drives the new year salmon through the quarry pool.

Mr P. is open before nine and the door bell rings steadily. Old friends. People simply looking in, some to buy a fly or two as a passport to talk with the man. It is a den. It has intimacy and warmth compared with city tackle emporiums, it is a fisherman's shell.

He has been out all night, or if not that, he took only an hour or two of sleep sometime after dawn. Last night, he was a man alone out there on the river in the moors, totally absorbed in his art, in his life's challenge and in his puzzles. He long ago perfected the laying of noiseless line over shallows only six inches deep. He has immersed himself so long in the life of the river that he knows it as well as a man can. Still, every night, he will have to play the game over: with big flies, small flies, sunken flies, surface flies, flies worked, lifted or left to drift, until he finds what and where and how the trout are wanting them that moment in time. The Eden has more options than a chessboard. It is a glass bead game played in the dark as the river flows past him with the starlight in its folds.

On his hand, he places one of his little wet flies, tiny and dark, a perfect river nymph. When the hackles are wet they lie back over the hook and the tips tangle and work in the current like the

[136]

antennae or legs of the real insect, that comes out after dark, that works over the river bed after his living.

Conditions had been perfect the night before. Feather cloud formations so that the face of the nearly full moon was visible but its brightness muted; so that there was enough light to fish well, to plan every footfall, stalk like a night heron, and yet there was enough cover to seal in the warmth of the day; so that the Eden olives and sedges were encouraged to hatch on every hour to dawn and beyond.

Even so, it had been a hard night for fishing, but almost, that was so much the better, for so the challenge was greater. See that stooping black figure wading the flats of the river, moving, but imperceptibly, without ripple or sound, more a wraith than a man. Yet, the gentle hiss of his line sometimes hangs in the air, but the splashing, the rising of fish around him continues. They are oblivious to him, uncaring, almost, whether they are caught.

Through flat after flat he wanders, searching fish after fish; his concentration never fails, his mind never ever leaves the dark river, the singing shallows, the polished pools. And when, in the world of black and silver, the trout do come on to his flies they will do so breath-takingly sharply, as though they yearned to die at his hands alone.

Then he feels the plucks or the tugs that excite him so and draw him back there night after lonely night and though he will never know all, so he will never fall out of love with the Eden.

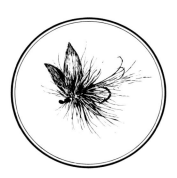

A House by a Pool
on the Tweed

There is a house on the banks of the Tweed where I have always found myself at peace, in total sympathy for all that surrounds it. Whatever the season, no matter how the night winds blow, I dream of my life being played out there, very happily, totally absorbed in everything the great border valley offers.

It is single storey, of stone, with a slate roof, bedded twenty feet up from the summer river level. Whenever the sun glimpses through, a cat appears on the doorstep. Chickens run round the yard, through the sheds, in and out of the orchard and a dog barks at strangers who venture down the track. Smoke whisps from the chimney in curlyways up the hillside. The view is across the river, to Scotland, of forests, sandstone cliffs and thickly sheeped grassland.

In the winter, the house gives the only light for miles both up and down the valley. The violence of the power drive river stops just short of its doors but the winds that shriek round the gables cut to the bone and the frosts that settle on the roof are wicked ones. On a still night, hear a vixen cry at you from Scotland, see deer tracks fresh in the overnight snow, and when the moon is up over the water the salmon thread upriver, stitching like silver needles as they leap. Nowhere is more an angler's house, close to the endless song of the falls, light as a choirboy's in the summer, but a growling bass from the first floods on when, for some, it would become a bleak dwelling.

Today a man salmon fishes there, wading almost to his chest in

[139]

a deep push of water. His long rod catches the sunlight and around him the line whirls and lassoes, before he lets it go like an arrow, again, to where the fish are. Sometimes fish jump, angry at the low water, wasting their strength in senseless splashes of impatience at the now weak river. Between the man and England, where the river is only a foot deep, there is a steady rise of brown trout, just within range of the two piece, if I do not hurry it but let it work to its own rhythm.

But it is the pool that fascinates me the most, that has the most possibilities, that throbs with life of every sort. The pool that lies slightly upstream of the house gives the whole place its spell of

drama. Perhaps it is more an eddy than a pool, created as the main force of the river is thrown off a promontory of rocks and funnelled against the northern bank, leaving on the south a deep, mysterious slack. In area it is an acre, perhaps two, twenty feet deep and more in the plunging crevasses. Only superficially is it placid, in reality it is veined with currents, that seem to conflict, but actually combine into finely interwoven patterns that all manner of fish adapt to. Imagine the pool like a muscle on the river, seeming still, but rippling with sinew, full of life and vigour.

It is hardly a lie, for it is large enough, independent enough to claim an existence in its own right. The pool is a world of its own with its own creatures that need never leave it for the river. It is a water jungle of currents, of life, of depths shot through by glimmers of light, of bubbles and foam and pastures of weed.

[140]

There are monsters there, and travellers, and little fish and big ones and the man who lives in the house can watch it all happen beneath him.

A big she-pike lives there. So richly has she fed that she is near forty pounds and never once has she left the eddy. She hardly realises that she is a river fish, only that it brings to her door fresh salmon, when she might fancy them. Fish that stay over for heavy water; or because in the summer they like those strange currents that push and pull at their flanks and remind them of the sea; or because the pool is so alone and is so rarely netted or fished that racial memory recommends it as a safe haven. But a salmon has to be large to escape the pike if she wishes one, and even twenty pounders she has mauled across the belly before they have broken free only to bleed and roll away in the currents.

The pike knows all the paths through the rock forest and where the prey fish cluster to escape when they feel her coming, like a wolf through the dark. The flock she seeks out and harries before her is the roach shoal of the pool, five hundred fish strong, that roams the mid water vastness, aware of the pike beneath, following with her eyes, nosing up from her dungeons, eager to add an easy two pounds more to her bulk.

With the fish across her jaws, spilling scales like confetti, she descends to her lair, turns the roach and slowly swallows it. Does she taste it, does satisfaction enter that primitive brain? A trout is so obviously excited in a good rise, but for her the thrill is dulled and gone. The thing the pool so fears does no more than exist, alone, a death machine, without passion or joy, in some role the creator of the pool spelled out for her.

When it is dawn and still, perhaps with mist veiling the weak sunrise, a troupe of dorsal fins cuts the shallows on the lip of the great pool. The fin rays reach out sharp and erect from the tissue, as if a porcupine were somehow cruising there just underwater. Shoals of small fishes continually shower away in front of the danger point, some are chased and engulfed in the growing water bulge. The buccaneers are about, the Jolly Rogers, the saw-toothed dorsals are their flag. The perch: their backs are barred with black, their fins are flaming red, the bully boys of the pool,

always roaming, an eye to the main chance and a mouth big enough to engulf it, whatever it is. They will have a fish a third of their own weight, head first and hit the water lanes again; after trouble once more, after the babies of the place, the dace or the gudgeon; or to beat up a shoal of parr, perhaps; they will even harass the minnows of the place, the twitching, finch–like fingerlings of the water world. When you are a rogue, or a perch, any booty will do so long as your belly is full enough to let you sleep at night.

That day started with a drizzle, Scottish drizzle, born out of bogs, drifted in on a slight northerly breeze. Drizzle, dense as fog, drowned the valley in silence and gloom: it dampened the very heart. The sky and the drizzle were as one. The air was water and to breathe was almost to drown. Every rheumatic joint developed over a quarter of a watery century responded. I was in water, beside water: a drizzle freckled Tweed ran inches beneath my water boots. The reel was sodden and crotchety: the rod was no more than a damp, dripping reed: the line clung when it should have flown. I was wading the shallows down the pool. Feeling alone, but happy I was so. Until. . .

Out of the mists shrouding the Scottish shore, arose a bow-wave, a wall of water a yard high. It travelled with pace and precision. The river stopped for it and so did my heart. In that half light, I felt menaced by the eruption that veered with chilling accuracy to the gravels on which I stood. I believed and I could not believe, for surely I was angling on a placid British river, just where a man should never be afraid.

At ten yards, the pivot, the moving force of the surge, became visible as a shape, both long and black, driving the water before it, towards me, relentlessly through the haze into my night-mares. Only at my boots did the apparition turn and as the wave swelled to my waist, so upped the head of a seal, polished, black and bald, but for a clutch of drooping whiskers. And I swear his eyes were laughing, little coal pits of fun.

The pool, for both of us, meant fish, and was vast enough to provide for our wants. So it was, we caught what he needed and what I wanted and we stayed on together for days until he would sleep on the rocks whilst I stood quiet beside him, almost over him.

As a seal, he seemed just as happy with roach or grayling as trout, and even more so with eels. The river was low for salmon, he had no desire for perch and I reckon he kept away from the she-pike, so all in all we trod on neither's toes. It was only later I heard he had swum the lower beats for weeks, breaking up salmon nets, taking big fish in front of ghillies and anglers, generally creating havoc. Fury had followed his flippers my way, but perhaps he holed up with me just long enough on the pool for men to forget, to open up his way back home again, to the sea.

The Till

By the time I got to the far North of England, it was well into September and summer was paling. Its going was grimly apparent to me: the closing down of evenings into longer nights: heavier dews and stay-a-bed dawns: a sun less warm and winds more keen: colours jaded and lights less bright. Harvests everywhere were pretty well done with and, on the skylines, tractors ploughed in the stubble. There was a restlessness amongst the migrating birds and the rising of trout which, after that night on the Eden, became more erratic and less predictable. Though there were sure to be more good days, the bleak wind-swept depressions when the rain falls from dawn to dusk and beyond, were to be sniffed in the wind.

By me at least. Perhaps it was that the first retreats of the summer were made in my mind, and because I so dreaded its ending, I was in part looking for its going. I so feared losing its warmth, its rivers and the freedom it gave me; I was eager to cling to its remnants and was equally aware of signs of its surrender to the passing of time.

So, on one of my rare trips home, I sensed rather than saw the bracken draw back and felt the trees to be on the turn, their leaves dying and becoming brown. The old man in the garden talked about getting in the last of the potatoes and remarked that the lawns needed cutting less and less. He was looking to mend the roofs on the sheds before the gales got under them, was wondering if the track would survive another season of the frosts and snows that he too was well aware of, that seemed to grin over his bowed shoulders.

[145]

By the pond there was a toad, barely moving, with maggots working in its empty eye sockets. It fell on its back, showed its flaccid stomach and could not recover any balance however it waved its limbs. I killed it with a stone and it sank slowly into the depths by the dam where the sticklebacks would dart on it.

It was the Till that led me out of this unusual depression, with its beauty and with the fineness of the estate around its valley. Northumberland is immortal landscape.

Everyone was on the boats, out on the slack river. Anglers and water both were tired and despondent. No one went out until mid morning and all were back early in the afternoon, for on a river so low, spirits just die. Some even paid their bills and left southwards. Those that remained had no current to work a fly in, but no depth and far too much weed for a spinner either. Blanket weed was everybody's nightmare. Occasional salmon were seen, the majority long in the river; and there were some reddened sea trout, but you could only feel sorry for these and hardly fish for them.

It is easy to tell a fishing hotel in despondency, its lack of bubble and excitement, and everyone had autumn on his mind, when the rain would come. The big spates were only days or weeks off, when the fresh salmon would run against the surge of white water. All the beats were booked, the boats taken, and the hotel was full in anticipation of the coming big fish. As for now,

the ghillies would rather have been off the river, working on their boats, looking to their vegetable gardens or doing anything in preparation rather than be idle in frustration.

So, I went my own way, leaving the heavy gear and taking up the two piece again, to walk the lower Till where nothing was dictated to me, glad to be free again, to roam, to fish or sit just as I wanted. I was back into the spirit of my travels as I went down the valley, at first narrow and steep sided, dark with trees but which opened out into rolling hills and splendour at the confluence of Till and Tweed.

If there is any place in the whole wide world that God has created in the fashion of Heaven itself, has painted with all the shades of grace and beauty, then it is surely that point where the two rivers meet. They join behind a great island that shelters the scene from the savage north winds; they are overlooked by the remains of a chapel that He allowed to be built in his honour, to bless their union, in the wilds far from any man, on those last few yards of English soil. There is beauty still on the tumbled walls, on the trees that He has cared to grow up the hillsides, in the wildfowl that He rears to cross and recross the great border river, in the salmon He drives through the depths of winter and in the brown trout with which He rejoices and decorates the gravel beds.

And also, in the last of His blizzards and storms, He caused a grayling swim to be created in the eye of this paradise, on the very bend of this lovely junction, just where the mighty stream meets the lesser under gracefully weeping trees. And if the salmon is the king of this heaven, and the trout is his queen, then the grayling is surely her closest handmaiden.

I was alone there. The sand beach had no footprint upon it. The fisherman's hut was secured and the padlock lay long rusted, unused in the loneliness of that place. A misty afternoon was merging with the dusk and in no more than half light, I knelt on the sand and cast to the point where the Till ran out, rapidly over a long gravel bar, before delving into the larger river. It was as long a cast as I could easily make, upstream, but sweeping down, opposite and finally beneath me, the line moving like the second hand of an enormous watch face. When it had reached the one o' clock mark, or thereabouts, I had the inkling of a something, a passing belief that the fly was not alone in the world any longer. I felt no tug, no take, the line did not halt or move upstream and there was no sensation through the rod which had become to me as sensitive as a cricket's antenna.

I did not know, I was not sure, but on the second cast I was more careful to lay down a whisp of a line, alert there on the sand, peering over the darkening river, oblivious to the mist that had developed into a fine rain. And, when the cast was at the point of noon, the same experience, inchoate and intangible, prickled along my spine and I struck quite wildly into nothing at all.

Casts merged into each other and the shallows seemed quite fishless after all, until once more the rod and the line began to tingle for me, like the forked willow whispers water to the diviner's touch. No gleam though, no bulge, there was nothing more than these hints, these fantasies in the twilight. Twilight; later than that and with the valley too dark and wet to continue, I strayed homewards.

I was the only angler in the hotel that night who looked forward to the following day because I was the only one with a secret, with a challenge facing, with any real prospect of success ahead of me. Nagging doubts had chased me all along the valley way home, fears that the fish I suspected were only cheating ribbons of weed whose duplicity would be revealed by the next morning's daylight. But deep down, I knew that the species I had brushed with were grayling.

The world being as it is, I knew my hopes of grayling would excite interest or enthusiasm in very few of the bar grumblers, so I kept my find quiet, knowing I would be the only angler to set an alarm, or to order an early breakfast, or to dream in the heavily curtained bedroom of glinting fish and clear running rivers.

My passion for grayling hardly suffered from the walk to the Till–Tweed confluence very early the next morning. The dew lay in an unbroken sheen along the path; the flights of duck rose up in curtains as I approached and the rabbits could hardly believe their sleep starved little eyes. Where the fir trees pressed in, I tore

[148]

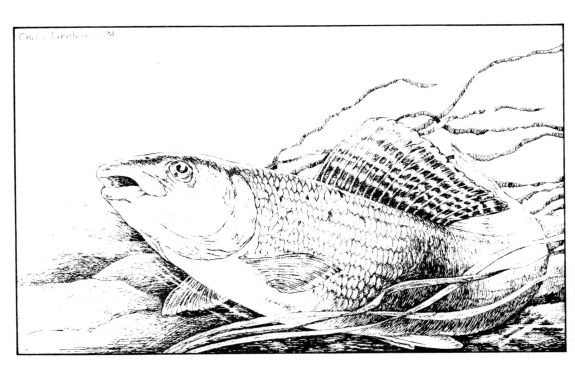

the silver beaded spider webs and where the valley widened out, I frightened off the heron wading beneath the railway bridge.

The river was cold as I searched it, turning over its stone lined bottom, hunting out the food store of the gravels. Water fleas for the most part, small shrimps, several snail families, nymphs in plenty and many caddis. Looking at the squirming samples in my hand, I felt a small dark pheasant tail was as fair an imitation of any of these blob lives as anything else. I kneeled again in the sand.

My first cast of the new day snaked out, and as before bellied with the flow. I watched the leader along every knot, over every boulder with a burning intensity for action – that came so fast, so dramatically that the take of the fish could be heard, quite loud as it slashed the line tight through the water. It was a second from every man's season when a fish is on, suddenly, magically, and all one can do is give slack as to a fleeing devil.

The fish was plunging, revolving on to its back, gleaming its slim yellow belly, hanging in the current, arrowing away in short thrusts and rattling the rod tip. Yard by yard the two piece worked it into the shallows, where it swam higher in the water, where the proud dorsal of a big grayling extended. I could watch her fight in the now sunlit, clear water.

This has always been an aspect of fishing that I cherish, I like to think, not because of cruelty, but because the fish is displayed at its best. Now the grayling had her fins erect, her gills were flaring, her whole body was working as she fought the thin strand of nylon. It was the same thrill as watching straining athletes, or the foam flecked racehorse, or a swan in those first few beats of flight. I was in awe of the beautiful; I was fascinated by the physical. None of us know about the morality of what we do, but I do feel my presence on rivers this summer has done little harm. And if I do not praise the grayling, fight for her as much as against her, few others will do so in my stead.

I unhooked that fish without even taking her from the water, simply by letting her lie on her side on the waterline, washed up and down by the still rippling shallows; in her own element she looked natural, retained that beauty of any wild creature at bay that is still untouched, bred not by man's design, but despite him.

Her pectoral and ventral fins were golden yellow, but the latter was marbled with brown over the gold, looking like the breast of a thrush caught in a shaft of sunlight. Her eye was ringed deep with gold. Most beautiful, her top three rows of scales, from her tip to her tail, caught now the light from the sky, then the reflections from the water and glistened in turn with shifting silvers, blues and purples. And most strange, on each flank, parallel to each other from the head to the ventral fin, ran two golden lines, as though traced in gold-dust, by an angel.

I was looking at colours that no-one but an angler ever sees, that exist nowhere else in the world but on these remarkable, too little sought after fish. Colours that were caught in the nether land between water and air.

I had contacted a big grayling shoal and over the next days I

[150]

took over a dozen different fish, and one or two more than once. Each morning I set off in a jog down the valley and the salmon men stared at my going, wondering at such happiness in such gloom.

My style of fishing produced takes that made my blood freeze. I was, almost, trotting the flow like a float man on the Trent after roach or gudgeon. I worked the fly hard, lifting it, or holding it back enough to bring a grayling in on it with a barnstorming lunge, zipping the line tight, violent as a sea trout.

Of course, the body of the shoal moved, not from the beat entirely, but up and down it along a rough hundred yard run. Ideally, I began at the head of the gravels, working water until I contacted the fish.

After I had been given two or three chances, or fish, the shoal moved once more, and so would I, downstream until I found them, or failing that, I would return to the top of the run once more. I did not make a drudge of it. I let the fish settle between times whilst I read, or drank a drop, or watched the valley life roll by. But, I could not let it alone too long, enthralled by the magic of those takes, always on edge, waiting for that bolt from the blue water. This, combined with the beauty of the grayling and the riverscape was all I could ever wish for.

Faustus proved a bad man can fly to the Poles, or hide in the jungles, but hell will go with him. Equally, I like to think that this special place has been with me since, forcing me to look more at the good things of life. Certainly I have never been more grateful since I became an angler. Whether we fish the Tweed, the Test, or the Thames, we are men and women apart from our fellows.

The last cast that I made this summer was over those grayling, but they had finally wised up to me and begun to break up, much like the summer. Those that did not disperse, those I did drift a fly over, had seen me before and I could not raise a fish.

I climbed the steep hill south of the the junction and took a last look at the summer I was about to step out of. A brown hare stood astonished to see me and when I sat down, he moved merely five yards before eating once again. The whole scene stretched out in front of me: the chapel, the island, the Till, the Tweed, England, Scotland, the water and the sky, all part of a glorious whole. And it is this vision I have now in my mind when people ask why I fish: because nowhere else in life do beauty, challenge, excitement and deep understanding combine so precisely for me. It has been in this spirit I have tried to tell the tale of these travels.

Conclusion

Suppose, now at the end, I let the statistics speak? I drove a little over 2,400 miles, through, I believe, twenty-one counties. I broke down twice, both times on the hills of Devon. I caught fifteen sea trout, 124 brown trout, six rainbows, twenty-four grayling, three perch, two chub, one gudgeon, five dace and several minnows that dropped off just over the bank. The biggest was a sea trout just under six pounds but perhaps the most notable was a grayling edging just over two pounds. The longest fight lasted for fifteen minutes. I lost five well hooked fish, one through a faulty hook knot and four in snags.

The biggest fish I saw alive was a pike in the Tweed that was well over thirty pounds. The largest I saw dead was a twenty-eight pound salmon rowed in on the Borders and the largest I saw cased was the forty pounder in the lobby of the Tillmouth Park Hotel. The strangest fish I saw or caught was on the Lyd. Even with photographs, two pages of description I wrote at the time, and with three guides to European fishes, I still cannot place it.

To my knowledge, I only killed one fish. I would like to think that the remaining 180 odd survive, and breed to produce ten times that number so that rivers will flourish, stocking needs reduce, prices will come down, and more men will be able to afford days of bliss. I nearly killed myself once, falling into the Tamar.

I returned having bought or made 109 flies of differing local patterns. I did record losing seventeen flies, five in fish, I am afraid. I do not know how many times I cast, but the blisters that formed, and burst, have since hardened over and made my right hand horny as a road mender's.

I wore through two pairs of water boots. I estimate I walked between 500 and 550 miles during the ten weeks, at about seven miles a day, along sixteen rivers and their sidestreams. I destroyed one pair of trousers and one thigh-boot on barbed wire and I had trouble with two bulls.

I slept in thirteen different beds, one night in a river hut and several times on the bank. When I was questioned in Berwick on Tweed by a lady researcher as to how many bottles of wine I had drunk in the month past, I frightened her!

I fished on sixty-three days and fished right through eight nights. I poached, by mistake, once, and swore more often. The weather was astounding. I saw the sun everyday. I picked up my best tan for sixteen years. I was caught in three storms. I was rained on, briefly, another four times. Winds were fresh or strong on six occasions.

I saw several buzzards, harriers, sparrowhawks and a great many kestrels, owls, grebes and jays, magpies and herons just about everywhere. I had a squirrel eat my lunch on the Barle. I saw deer, totally wild, in three places, and one otter and one badger sett, and though I waited, the occupant did not show. I saw five foxes, three alive and two on a keeper's line.

On all but three ventures after medium to large sea trout, I used the one rod, the two piece, which I needed to mend three times. I harnessed it generally to just the one floating line, a No. 6 double taper which served me almost everywhere. The heaviest cast I attached was seven pounds, and the lightest a decimal point over one pound. The largest fly was tied to a size 8 and the smallest to a size 22. The most frequently used was a pheasant tail nymph on either size 14 or 16 but floating Olive imitations were a close second.

I saw three brilliant anglers on my travels, and spoke to several I expect were as good. I learnt much from eight river keepers and four gems of tackle shop dealers. My hosts were uniformly generous. I like to think that I made no enemies and perhaps some friends.

And why did I do it all? Because I had one father who died rather young on a stormy winter's night, in a draughty house that overlooked the windswept North Sea and who told me in his three last sentences to treasure summer days and above all, to try to do what my heart will tell me to.

'You have,' he said, 'only one life.' And that, coming at the last, in the face of the void, really was an instruction.

Epilogue
The Fragility of Rivers

In the spring this year the Committee of the River Glaven received a letter, unsolicited, from one of its most enthusiastic members. It was headed 'Fishing: 19 May 1984' and it read:

'It was a warm, sunny day with very little wind. At high tide, conditions could not have been more perfect.

I fished the river from Wiveton Bridge to Savory's Marsh for about two hours in the morning and one and a half hours in the evening, putting seven hours at work in between.

I used a No. 7 double tapered floating line, a twelve foot, three pound leader, and a No. 12 Mallard and Claret fly I tied many years ago – 1963 to be precise! The hook was rusty and the wings and the golden pheasant tippets had long since come off in the passage of time.

My first fish was taken just below the dam, upstream of Wiveton Bridge. An extremely fit brown trout of two and three-quarter pounds which took between fifteen and twenty minutes to net – the longest I have ever had to play a fish, but the aged hook and light leader were constantly on my mind.

Casting upstream, I netted a further twenty-four brownies around half a pound each and all were returned to the river. There had been virtually no rain for ten weeks and the water, except at high tide, was so low there were large areas of barely submerged mud close to the bank which made the netting and returning of fish difficult, to say the least.

[157]

At dusk I lost my twenty one year old fly, not on a fish but on a nettle, so I decided to call it a day. But, I ask you, what a day!'

A month or so later I netted another good brown for the writer of the letter, John Oxenford, on another glorious evening. However, in August, I received another letter, this time from Peter Suckling, Secretary of the Club.

RIVER GLAVEN FISHERY ASSOCIATION
Cley Next the Sea,
Norfolk.

6th August 1984

Dear John,

Last week the river was fishing the best it has done for three years but there has been an excessive build up of weed. The water level above our fishery was too high and threatened the fish farm. Arrangements had to be made with me to cut the weed and it was necessary to remove the boom (just above Wiveton Bridge) to allow the Anglian Water boat to pass. Last Wednesday there was a serious spillage of diesel oil into the Glaven some four miles above our stretch. As a result to this threat of pollution the weed cutting had to be done in great haste. Our fishing stretch has been ruined.

Having surveyed the river today it would appear that we have lost all the fish and the river is quite unfishable and will remain so for the rest of this season. In October the stretch between Wiveton Bridge and Glandford will be dredged and there seems to be no point in either replacing the boom or restocking the river.

I am making representations and will advise you in due course of the outcome.

Yours sincerely,
Peter Suckling.

When I got to the river it became obvious that the three years of work the Association had put into the river had been set back considerably. In its haste to cut the weed, to hasten the flow and flush the diesel out to sea, the weedcutter had removed our weirs, destroyed the groynes, uprooted the weed types we had introduced and had left, if such a thing is possible, a desert of water.

The trout stocks that we were justly proud of had suffocated in the silt and died, or surviving and finding no lies left, feeling themselves homeless, had gone downstream through the sluices and out to sea. No doubt most had perished there too, but a few found their way into the brackish creeks and dykes where they could grow very large on sea shrimps, baby flounders, elvers and the like.

Death is a sad, ugly thing. The attraction of a trout lies in its alertness, its balance, its leopard beauty and poise: a dead trout loses all these things. It hangs drunkenly in the silt. It becomes shapeless. The parasites move in on it. It rots. I preferred to think of the trout that might have escaped, might pirate a new career for themselves around the coast, might take on a silver sheen and live more like sea trout, perhaps to return to the river in future years if we get it right again.

In some moods I can admire herons, when they fish skilfully. But when they settle like the grey legions of death, they disgust me. Half eaten trout lay on the bankside. The toads that had scattered from the dying river had been picked off, most by the eyes, or by the choicest parts of their intestines. The only fish I saw alive were gudgeon, skittering here and there, unable to find cover on the wasteland river bed, frightened by a shadow and neurotic for a home.

Whilst I despaired for a lovely river lost, I felt soon after for those like John Oxenford who had enjoyed it most. I thought of Mr Savory who has such a closeness to the river. Whatever might be repaired in the future, whatever might still be for the Glaven, when once over eighty, how far do you rely on seeing each new spring?

Can I rely on the Committee to pick itself up and start the work of river rebirth, of lie construction all over again? Knowing

[159]

Peter Suckling, his energy and his buoyancy, I am pretty sure I can.

Perhaps the unkindest thing is that the diesel never got near our beat. It petered out miles upstream. The weed cut was not necessary. The river died totally in vain. Man's mistake. The fragility of rivers.

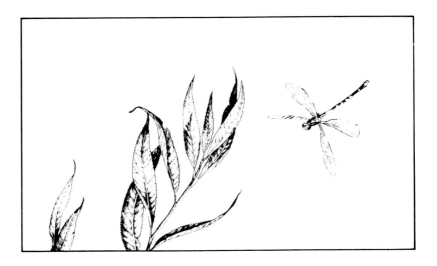